Manners and Meaning in West Sumatra

MANNERS AND MEANING IN WEST SUMATRA

The Social Context of Consciousness

FREDERICK K. ERRINGTON

Yale University Press
New Haven and London

Designed by Nancy Ovedovitz and set in VIP Bodoni type. Printed in the United States of America by BookCrafters, Inc., Chelsea, Michigan.

Library of Congress Cataloging in Publication Data

Errington, Frederick Karl.
  Manners and meaning in West Sumatra.
  Bibliography: p.
  Includes index.
    1. Minangkabau   (Indonesian   people)—Psychology.
2. Philosophy, Minangkabau (Indonesian people) 3. Minangkabau (Indonesian people)—Social life and customs. 4. Sumatera Barat (Indonesia)—Social life and customs.   I. Title.
DS632.M4E77   1984   306'.0899922   83-21893
ISBN 0-300-03159-9

10   9   8   7   6   5   4   3   2   1

To the Memory of
Paul Lester Errington

Contents

Illustrations

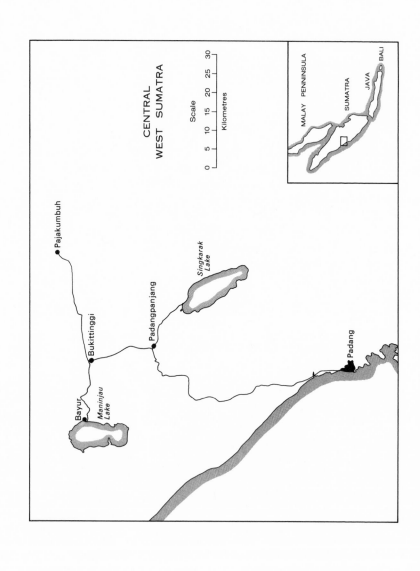

CENTRAL
WEST SUMATRA

Scale

0   5   10   15   20   25   30

Kilometres

Pajakumbuh

Bukittinggi

Bayur

Maninjau
Lake

Padangpanjang

Singkarak
Lake

Padang

MALAY PENNINSULA

SUMATRA

JAVA

BALI

Preface

The Minangkabau of West Sumatra are well known by anthropologists because they are strongly matrilineal yet staunchly Islamic and because their young men travel widely and work for protracted periods away from their home villages without losing a sense of distinctive cultural identity. Although these structural features of Minangkabau social life have stimulated several generations of anthropologists to write extensively about them (see especially the important recent books by Kahn, 1980; Graves, 1981; Phillips, 1981; Kato, 1982; and Dobbin, 1983), there has yet been no study of the system of meaning which sustains these social forms. My purpose in this book is to examine the cultural process through which the Minangkabau convince themselves that their social forms are not only distinctive but are right and proper.

In particular, I examine the central cultural ideas at work in this complex society and ask how Minangkabau concepts which purport to explain experience can remain valid when that experience is diverse and continually changing and how Minangkabau concepts can remain both intellectually and emotionally compelling under circumstances in which their meaning is subject to scrutiny, exegesis, and debate by local experts. The Minangkabau have developed a distinctive style of interpretation which allows them to resolve these problems of meaning, a style which they apply both in their evaluation of conduct—that is, in their etiquette—and in their explanation of social form generally—that is, in their understanding of their own customs. This monograph, thus, is an examination of Minangkabau indigenous epistemology.

It is also a reconsideration of the anthropological concept of

symbol. My examination of Minangkabau thought has led me to
reject the utility of this concept as an appropriate means of understanding Minangkabau consciousness. The Minangkabau are
able to construct and embody truth in their lives through a style
of interpretation which seeks and finds meaning displayed on the
visible surfaces of social action. Their preferred mode of interpretation is to focus on the relatively apparent rather than on the
obscure and hidden. Correspondingly, meaning for them is conveyed through signs rather than through symbols. Minangkabau
consciousness, which finds meaning to be conveyed through signs
rather than through symbols, is, therefore, in contrast to the Western consciousness of most anthropologists. Anthropologists, I
argue, must recognize that their cultural—and disciplinary—
preference to interpret through symbols may be inappropriate for
understanding the consciousness of non-Western groups such as
the Minangkabau. Through their reliance on the concept of symbol,
anthropologists may frequently be ethnocentric and distort the cultural experience of other groups through overinterpretation.

My research took place between February and July 1975. I
consider the data I collected during the six months I was allowed
in the field by the Indonesian government to be a reliable basis
for my interpretations in this book. Because the Minangkabau are
both extraverted and highly articulate, I was able during that time
to collect a considerable body of information. Moreover, conversations I had in the field and subsequently with anthropological
colleagues who were able to have more extended and, in some
cases, more recent stays with the Minangkabau confirmed my perception that my data were indeed representative. In addition, I
was able to see during my six months virtually all of the Minangkabau rituals, including the rare and supremely important ascension of a *panghulu*.

I did most of my fieldwork using the Indonesian language. Minangkabau and Indonesian are so close as languages that most of
the men and many of the women had virtually as little difficulty
in expressing themselves to me in Indonesian as in their native
Minangkabau. In most cases I have used actual names of persons

and places in the conviction that the people of Bayur would prefer for me to do so.

There are two areas in which my ethnographic knowledge is less complete than I would like. My knowledge of the role of Islam in Bayur would have been greater if I had been allowed to enter the community mosque and if I had been present in Bayur during the month of fasting. However, informants gave me extensive accounts of what I missed and I was able to get substantial information on popular Islam in Bayur through a variety of other ways. I did hear a number of sermons in several of the prayer houses and was told of yet others. I attended weddings, graveside funerals, memorial prayers, and participated in the community celebration of the Prophet's birthday. I also heard and was able to discuss with my informants the frequent references to Islam and the Koran that characterized official functions, communal and family gatherings, and everyday life. I was subject to arguments urging me to convert to Islam. In all of these contexts, the presentation and interpretation of Islam followed the same pattern of thought that is apparent in other aspects of Minangkabau life.

My data on the views held by women in Bayur are also incomplete because there are strict rules concerning the propriety of contact between the sexes. Although I was able to talk to a few women in detail about some aspects of their lives as Minangkabau and do have available one excellent account (Tanner 1971) which conveys considerable material about Minangkabau women, unfortunately, my own account is primarily from a male perspective.

My research was made possible by Amherst College. I wish to thank the Republic of Indonesia for its cooperation at the national, provincial, district, and local levels. I am particularly grateful to Lembaga Ilmu Pengetahuan Indonesia for its help in Jakarta and to Datuak Rajo Limo Koto, mayor of Bayur, for his extensive help in Bayur.

I wish to thank Kasfi Arsyad for introducing me to Bayur and for looking after my welfare while I was in West Sumatra. Yohannas Tanjung and Datuak Maleko were of immeasurable assistance to me in my research, as were Sutan Zara Endah, Dalius, Datuak Ramkayo Bungsu, Datuak Batuah, and Salma Machmud.

Nigel Phillips and Franz and Keebet von Benda Beckmann were

a source of friendship and ideas during my fieldwork. John and Ibi Molenveld and Peter and Barbara Schroeder were unfailingly hospitable.

A seminar on Southeast Asian Aesthetics given at the University of Michigan, June 1977 (sponsored by the Social Science Research Council and organized by Alton Becker and Benedict Anderson), proved an important source of ideas for me.

And finally, I wish to thank Joanne Prindiville, who provided me with important information, suggestions, and criticisms; James Siegel, Karl Heider, and Michael LeParte, each of whom carefully read my manuscript and offered helpful suggestions; and Carolyn Errington, who provided editorial help. Most of all I would like to thank Deborah Gewertz. I found her advice in the framing and organization of general arguments, as well as in the explication of particular points, to be invaluable.

Introduction
Cultural Preoccupations

How typical a Minangkabau was my companion, I wondered, as we squeezed into the bus to begin our six-hour trip to his home village of Bayur? How did the world look to him—what was the nature of his cultural perspective? Would he begin to reveal in conversation the preoccupations that might serve to introduce me to the nature of Minangkabau cultural experiences and cultural identity?

I had come to Indonesia to study the Minangkabau (also called the Minang), in part to understand how cultural identity was possible for members of a society who had experienced a long and varied history of cultural contact. It was my expectation that members of such a society, subject to a wide variety of influences, would be sufficiently self-conscious about their cultural identity to be able to talk explicitly about much of what they did and why. This research among the Minang, I hoped, would provide an effective contrast to my previous New Guinea fieldwork in the relatively encapsulated island society of Karavar, where meaning remained implicit, largely embedded in action. I was now ready to explore a different set of questions concerning how central cultural concepts work in complex societies: how those which purport to explain experience can remain valid when that experience is diverse and continually changing; how concepts can remain both intellectually and emotionally compelling under circumstances when their meaning is subject to open scrutiny.

The Minang were indeed a society which coupled a wide experience of other cultures with a reputation for cultural integrity and pride. They had, after all, been so influenced by Islam that they considered themselves to be among the staunchest Muslims of Southeast Asia; coastal Minang had been controlled by a distant Atjehnese sultan in the sixteenth century; Minang had long engaged in overland trade in gold and had imported goods by sea from as far away as the Maldives. (See Dobbin 1977 for an excellent and more complete discussion of the history of Minangkabau trade.) Moreover, and of most importance, they still preserved the long-standing practice of sending their young men to work outside of the Minangkabau homeland of West Sumatra—sending them on the *rantau*—with the explicit objective that these young men remain loyal Minangkabau while gathering information to bring back to their home villages about the cultural and social practices of the outside world. In this way, Minang villagers have for centuries received and then selectively assimilated a flow of information from all of Southeast Asia and, since the Minangkabau conversion to Islam in the sixteenth century, even from the Middle East.

My traveling companion certainly had experienced cultural diversity. He spoke some English, was entirely Westernized in dress, and was trained in economics. He was, in fact, a teacher of economics at several of the small universities in Padang, the provincial capital of the Indonesian province of West Sumatra. He also seemed to be strongly motivated by a sense of cultural identity and pride. During our fortuitous meeting near the Padang market, he had applauded my plan to study Minangkabau customs—I had been no more specific than that in our conversation—and he strongly argued that this project could very suitably be conducted in his home village. Although he admitted at the time we first met that he was not able to visit his village of Bayur very often, he nonetheless expressed pride in being a Minangkabau from Bayur. In this he seemed to conform to the Minangkabau reputation of being able to preserve at home and abroad a firm and personally sustaining sense of cultural origins.

At least I hoped he was still sufficiently Minang that I might begin to get an idea from him about the nature of the central and organizing concepts of Minang culture. I also hoped that his eagerness to cooperate with me would be typical of the Minangkabau of Bayur, although I recognized that chatting with me in the market or on a bus was rather different from having an anthropologist in residence, constantly poking his nose into other people's business.

The overloaded bus lurched through Bayur.

And, more specifically, I wondered how the people of Bayur would react to me in particular, given the Minangkabau experience of colonial rule and reputation for Islamic militancy. Would I even be able to investigate that blend of Islam and matrilineality for which they were already famous in the anthropological literature? Would my companion be able to facilitate my research under these potentially difficult circumstances? Was he still sufficiently a Minang to have remained credible to the members of his home village? If not, then my reception in Bayur might be even more difficult. Was I correct in thinking that at this stage of my research any introduction would be better than none?

What, I asked myself during these recurrent attacks of anxiety, was I doing lurching along in this overloaded bus as its bulging and bald tires splashed through the potholes of the uneven road leading from Padang into the highlands of the interior, the traditional heartland of the Minangkabau?

During the long trip my companion and I chatted as best we could in a mixture of Indonesian and English, each trying to practice the other's language, and I to get a better sense of what I might find in Bayur. I asked, for instance, whether Bayur had running water as much to use a carefully memorized Indonesian phrase as to get a sense of how remote the town might be. No, I was told, but the mosque did have electricity. As we proceeded into the highlands, threading our way through the traffic of motor-cycles, bicycles, two-wheeled carts pulled by water buffalo, and occasional trucks, cars, and buses, I could see fewer signs of prosperity. Houses were more likely to be unpainted and the roads more badly rutted. By the time the bus began its slow and very winding descent from the plateau through the steep upper zones of cultivated clove trees and then through the rice terraces of the more gentle lower slopes leading down to the crater lake of Man-injau and the nearby town of Bayur, I already had a good sense of what I would find. Throughout the trip, and especially on this last leg, I had been dazzled by the beauty of the landscape, which combined the soft greens and golds of the flat, maturing rice fields with the dark green of the jungles on the surrounding rugged hills. Along the lakeside approach to Bayur, these same contrasts between nature domesticated and wild were even sharper because of the intensely blue expanse of the lake and the extreme jaggedness of the mountains ringing it. Indeed, my companion told me, Minang and other Indonesians—and a few foreign tourists—sometimes vis-ited Lake Maninjau simply to enjoy this beauty.

As we entered Bayur I could see that it was in fact typical of the rural towns through which we had been passing. The highway constituting the main street was crowded with weathered and un-painted plank houses and small shops. If anything, Bayur was more crowded than most, since the side streets, stretching only a few hundred yards in each direction, ended at the lake on one side and the mountain slopes on the other. Bayur also had the same air of faded gentility which characterized many of the towns of the interior. In particular, I saw the same sprinkling of the large tra-ditional houses with carved ornamentation and upswept roofs. These roofs, I was told, replicated the shape of the horns of the Minang emblem, the water buffalo. But in Bayur, perhaps to a greater extent than in the towns we had passed through, many of these, as well as many of the smaller houses, had boarded-up windows

The gentle lower slopes lead down to the crater lake of Maninjau and the nearby town of Bayur.

Bayur had an air of faded gentility.

The traditional and now rather rare matrilineal house has an upswept roof representing the horns of a water buffalo.

and badly rusted corrugated iron roofs, suggesting that perhaps Bayur had experienced an unusually great decline from an earlier era of substantial prosperity and population.

Throughout the course of our trip, and in Bayur as well, the arrival of the bus created excitement. As our bus jolted through town, it blared out sprightly tunes on its battery of horns, as much to signal the importance of the occasion as to scatter any dogs and chickens wandering on the road. Our progress through Bayur was slow, giving me time to contemplate the mixture of excitement and dread I felt at actually arriving. The bus stopped, as it had all day whenever anyone wanted to get off. Getting off was rarely a simple procedure: it usually meant that a passenger clambered over half the occupants of the still crowded bus and then gave directions to the young men of the bus crew as they lifted down cardboard suitcases, bunches of coconuts, and crates of chickens acquired hours before at the regional market town. These crewmen obviously saw themselves as the center of attention during each stop. Smartly dressed in Western-style bell-bottomed trousers and platform shoes, they engaged in what appeared to be brisk repartee with each other

Getting off a bus in Bayur is rarely a simple procedure.

and with the local young men watching from the ground. Others, both men and women, gathered; some just to watch, some to greet the passengers.

Eventually the bus progressed the half-mile to the center of town, where my companion and I disembarked. The mayor's office was opposite from our bus stop and here a half-dozen men sat smoking and chatting on the porch. Adjacent was a school, its playground filled with noisy boys and girls, each wearing a relatively standard uniform of white shirt or blouse and blue shorts or skirt. A faded Indonesian flag hung slackly in the mid-afternoon heat. Just beyond was clearly the most impressive and well-maintained structure in town, the mosque.

The mayor himself wandered out, and my companion immediately introduced me to him. I explained somewhat baldly in Indonesian that I sought permission to live in Bayur so that I could learn about Minangkabau customs. My companion then provided a much more flowery—and, I think, effective—rendition of the same request, adding that I had authorization from Padang and Jakarta for this study. He then talked briefly with the mayor about some possible ways to bring economic prosperity to Bayur. I was

The mosque and adjacent mayor's office were clearly the most impressive
and well maintained structures in Bayur.

struck in these conversations, and in conversations later that
afternoon when we explained the purpose of my visit to other
older men, by their pervasive formality.

We stayed that first night with my companion's grandmother. I
was shown some of the family heirlooms—in particular, an elaborate cast-iron kerosene lamp suspended by chains from the
ceiling—and was told by her with quiet pride that in times past
lamps like this were fixtures in all Minang houses. The husband
of the grandmother (as he was called) seemed no more a part of
the household than the visitor who was my companion. In our
conversations with him, he said quite without enthusiasm that he
was planning to leave soon for the northern Sumatran city of Medan
because he had to earn some money to support himself. That he
was compelled to embark on this expedition by himself and at an
advanced age—he must have been in his sixties and did not appear
to be in especially good health—seemed to occasion no surprise.

My companion returned to work in Padang the next day, leaving
me with the assurance that it was all right for me to stay in Bayur.
In our final conversation, he said that he was glad enough to be

leaving but that he also found it of utmost importance to continue to visit Bayur periodically so that he would remain fully acceptable to the local Minangkabau. Being a Minangkabau male did not appear to be easy. Although my companion's educational accomplishments defined him as a success in the world, he seemed as little able to relax in Bayur, as little able to find a secure place there, as his grandmother's impoverished husband.

The mayor found me a place to room and board the next day across from his office, where he said he could look out for me. His sense of responsibility apparently was to the community at large: he wanted to make sure that my information about Minangkabau customs was accurate, and he also wanted to make particularly sure that I was not bothered by the youth whose rowdy behavior might give Bayur a bad name. I was not entirely certain that I wished to have my community contacts so carefully controlled and monitored, but at least my immediate needs were being taken care of. I was now free to begin thinking about the actual form my research should take. Although my statement upon arrival in Bayur that I wanted to study Minangkabau customs seemed to have been initially acceptable to its inhabitants, it now appeared distressingly vague to me. But in any case, no matter what my eventual focus, I would clearly need to begin to talk to Minangkabau in order to do any sort of fieldwork at all. Since the mayor had not actually suggested that I remain in my house, I began making forays on my own, heartened by the fact that there always seemed to be a great many men around who did not have anything obviously better to do than to talk to me.

As I wandered around town, I found myself accosted by boys and young men who hailed me with loud cries of "Hello, mister." In pursuing these conversational overtures, I discovered that this and "I love you" in most cases exhausted their supply of English. I also concluded that they were at least as interested in impressing their friends with their personal assertiveness and savoir faire as in having a conversation with me. I found such greetings rather jarring, and the older men also apparently regarded them as rude, for they made efforts to shush these youths.

Although the older men did not shout out to me in this way, I nevertheless sensed in their interactions with me a somewhat comparable interest in self-assertion. Whether in the form of the aggressiveness of the shouted greetings of the young men or in the tense formality of the older men, male conduct seemed to be characterized by confrontation. They asked me about who I was and why I was in their village in such a way as to emphasize their own personal significance. Few, if any, seemed to be occupied in mid-afternoon with anything other than conversation, an impression which began to fit in with my sense of setting. The shabby gentility of Bayur was of a piece with the rather tense, aggressive, and punctilious behavior of its men. Each contributed to a sense that social forms must be maintained; each suggested the idea that the men should be more important, active, and vital than they were. The relative idleness of so many of them appeared enforced, their leisure hardly relaxing.

My perceptions of the women were rather different. I certainly saw fewer women than men in public, and the older women in particular seemed to be busy with errands. They stopped and chatted with other women and, to some extent, with other men, but they had business to attend to and did not seem to share in the general male tension of enforced idleness. They evidently had a more secure, less assertive sense of themselves, at least as they appeared in public and, to judge from my encounter with my companion's grandmother, in private as well.

My initial impressions of Bayur were reinforced during the first weeks of wandering about trying to get a sense of the place and a clearer idea about what I should focus on. The Minangkabau themselves proved eager to explain some of these impressions by frequent reference to the circumstances in which Bayur—as well as many other Minang communities—now found itself.

These circumstances were rooted in the kind of cultural adaptation Bayur has been able to make to economic, demographic, and political changes of the twentieth century—changes that have in the last several decades, in particular, caused an important shift in the relationship of the home community to the outside world. Although Minang communities have, I knew, for generations sent their young men abroad to seek experience and fortune, only in the last several decades (with a dramatic increase in population and the failure of West Sumatra's right-wing rebellion against the

Sukarno government in 1958) has the outside world had to absorb such strikingly great numbers of Minangkabau. Indeed, according to figures I saw posted in the mayor's office, figures often cited to me in round numbers, Bayur had (in 1973) 4,511 persons actually in residence and 13,533 living elsewhere—mostly outside of West Sumatra—who still claimed Bayur as home. Minang, I subsequently learned, do tend to exaggerate the numbers of their community living abroad (Naim 1973), but in the absence of my own data I came to consider the mayor's figures plausible. They were at least more conservative than those of some, which ran as high as 50,000. Whatever the precise figure, the evidence was immediately obvious to all that a large number of those who would have composed the normal population of Bayur were absent. This was supported by my initial observation, readily confirmed by the people of Bayur, that many houses were either unoccupied or were only partially occupied. In addition, it was frequently noted that there was a disproportionate number of old people in the community.

That so many of its citizens were abroad was conveyed to me both as a source of pride and as a source of concern: pride in that it showed a high degree of individual enterprise, and concern in that it pointed to the extent of local economic stagnation and the threat to civic vigor.

The people of Bayur had come to have a clear and growing feeling that the real centers of vitality and significance were elsewhere. Most of the older men in the village, as I had first suspected, had little to do: many were entirely unemployed, subsisting on small pensions if they had been in government service or on stipends sent by children working in more economically active parts of Indonesia. They spent their days sitting in barely functional shops lining the main road, watching the traffic or the shop proprietor serve an occasional customer, stitch an occasional garment on his treadle machine, or give a haircut to an occasional patron. These men talked to each other and to me with considerable pride— and I suspected with some exaggeration—about the prosperity and professional status of their children in Jakarta or some other center. Certainly, though, they were not really happy with their own situations. Once one blurted out to me, "And we sit here in the village just getting stupid."

In a tailor shop a man remarked, "And we sit here in the village just getting stupid."

The young men in Bayur were scarcely more content. Those in their mid-teens bided their time until they could convince their parents that they had been in school long enough and were already sufficiently resourceful to make their way abroad. They felt an urgent need to get out from under the scrutiny of the community and of their mother's brother—their *mamak*—to experience the excitement and independence of life in the city, to collect their own stories of hard times endured and obstacles surmounted, to acquire city-wise ways and flashy Western-style clothing to display when they returned with the rest to Bayur in time for the celebration that climaxed the annual Muslim month of fasting. They wanted to make a name for themselves as men experienced and seasoned by the world. For those still planning to marry in Bayur, experience, or at least money earned, might be useful in eliciting a marriage proposal from the family of the prospective bride; for all, simply to have gone abroad was to be grown up, to have gone through a rite of passage. And, as in the past, because these youths were too restless for anyone's comfort and because the village itself was eager to learn what was happening in the wider world, they were encouraged to go.

The young women in Bayur were described to me as preoccupied with finding husbands, a pursuit becoming increasingly difficult as more and more men stayed abroad for longer periods. Prospective husbands had become sufficiently elusive that young women now were often sent abroad by their parents (to live with relatives, of course) or to continue their education. Sometimes they were stashed away in a religious school where they would be kept out of trouble; or sometimes they just languished in the village. Parental standards for a daughter's husband seemed to be relaxing, too: an acceptable husband no longer had to be from Bayur; he did not even have to be a Minangkabau; he did not even have to be a Muslim if he was willing to convert. And parents were becoming used to the idea that the couple might not dwell within easy view. Instead they might live in some distant city.

Moreover, many of the young and middle-aged men—those actually making their living in Bayur as artisans, shopkeepers, fishermen, and rice farmers—frequently talked about going abroad and often did, for months at a time. For example, one matrilineage titleholder—a *panghulu*—in his forties, was simultaneously photographer, tailor, and rice farmer when I arrived in Bayur. A few months later he took his wife and children to the distant Sumatran city of Medan and, after working there a few months in a shop, returned to Bayur to seek his living, at least for a while.

When I expressed surprise that rice cultivation did not occupy more of the men of Bayur, I was told that few found it inviting. Although it was still recognized as an occupation of fundamental importance, and control of rice land was still considered the ultimate security for old age, most agreed that growing rice not only was very hard work but was rather low in prestige since, for reasons tied into patterns of land tenure and social organization, it offered little opportunity for initiative and real economic success. Most of Bayur's men—whether junior or senior, whether part of a wealthy matrilineal family or not—did not, I discovered, themselves control rice land. If they worked rice land at all they did so as sharecroppers. The usual sharecropping arrangement was an even division of the crop, and most Bayur men have come to aspire to more than what would be only a subsistence living. It was the Minang women, particularly the senior women, who controlled the

Most agreed that growing rice offered little opportunity for initiative and real economic success.

use of matrilineally inherited land and houses. Sisters divided such an estate equally, to the complete exclusion of brothers. (Most Minang regard their practices pertaining to matrilineal inheritance as one of the few areas in which they are not staunchly in accord with Islamic prescription.) Although a mother's brother does have some authority over his sister's children, my informants insisted that he does not control his adult sisters, much less his mother, or the property they hold. Only if a man has purchased the land himself or has inherited in the absence of any sisters does he actually control the land. So reluctant are most Bayur men to work other people's land that sharecroppers must now be actively sought from other villages and given inducements such as access to coconut trees and free housing.

That so many in Bayur now find it either necessary or preferable to work abroad is, in the opinion of some of its more educated citizens, only the culmination of an early and unusually strong dependence on the outside world. This early dependence they in turn attribute to Bayur's physical setting. The town is not only closed in between Lake Maninjau and a surrounding range of mountains; it is also on the periphery of Agam, one of the three inland plateau districts comprising the traditional Minangkabau heartland. Because of its circumscribed land resources and its relatively remote location, Bayur was not settled until the 1840s.[1] Even when wet rice cultivation was supplemented in the twentieth century by hillside crops—first coffee, currently cloves—land resources proved inadequate to support an expanding population. In addition, I suspect that Bayur and its lakeside neighbors may have been too distant from the centers of trade to develop the village craft specializations which still characterize the more centrally located Minang plateau communities. In any case, they have responded by turning to the outside world as an increasingly important source of employment.

The people of Bayur told me with pride that their early dependence on the outside world has made Bayur and the other Lake Maninjau villages unusually progressive—concerned with social mobility, education, and Islamic reform. They supported this view by noting that the famous novelist and Islamic scholar and reformer, Hamka, and his father were from a neighboring Lake Maninjau village. Although the people of Bayur conceded that the gap has narrowed between Bayur and all but the most isolated Minang villages, they still regard their town as a center for reformist religious studies. Furthermore, they suggested that their community has a particularly strong commitment to the outside world not only as a source of livelihood but as a source of progressive ideas.

This pride has become somewhat tempered of late, however, because the experience of going abroad has clearly been changing in nature. No longer is it primarily a relatively brief transitional period for young bachelors; instead, many men expect to spend most of their working life—and perhaps their retirement as well—abroad with their families. It is recognized as a sad fact of contemporary life that many of those who have grown up in Bayur will in their turn raise children who might see Bayur, if at all, for only a few weeks each year.

The influence of the outside world has become inescapable. Not

1. This estimate is based on the research of a locally born political scientist, Dr. Haspi, and was communicated to me by him.

only are more citizens of Bayur experiencing more of the outside world by going abroad and staying longer, but, I eventually learned, the outside world itself has been impinging more and more directly on the community during the last one hundred and fifty years. West Sumatra began to come under colonial control when the Dutch (in 1821) intervened during the Padri War on behalf of the Minangkabau royal family against the forces of violently orthodox Islam. After a protracted struggle, during which virtually the entire royal family were killed, the Dutch gained effective control of West Sumatra.[2] (No currently available accounts exist which clearly indicate the nature of the dealings of the royal family with Minangkabau villagers.) Bayur has thus experienced the powerful presence of outsiders for about as long as it has existed. The Dutch were followed by the Japanese, who were followed by representatives of the postindependence Republic of Indonesia, often Javanese.

At the time of my research, Bayur's local government was on the national model, with a semi-elected mayor and a municipal secretary, who were responsible to a subdistrict, district, and provincial administration. Although these two municipal officials were from Bayur, they had to contend with much more than just local pressures. Similarly, the local schools and the local militia were all part of much wider organizations. Moreover, in recent years Western tourists have begun to pass through Bayur; people now listen to national and international news on the radio at home or outside shops, or read it in locally distributed newspapers.

This, then, was Bayur as I first encountered it, and the way I first began to make sense of some of my early impressions. The people of Bayur indeed seemed as concerned as I was curious about why there were so many absent from their community and so little to do for those who remained. But as I thought about these questions and began to understand them essentially as the Minangkabau did, I realized that although I was gaining an understanding of the circumstances in which their culture found itself,

2. Schrieke 1955 and Abdullah 1971 and 1972 are particularly good sources of information about the Dutch administration in West Sumatra: its taxation policy, coffee monopoly, policy toward lineage title holders and religious scholars, and so on.

I was still fundamentally unclear about the nature of their culture itself. There were, to be sure, many cultural details I could ask about; obviously much more was going on than I yet understood. Clearly I needed to find out more about social organization, the nature of the relationship between males and females—especially between husbands and wives—the nature and importance of Islam, and so on. But where to start and why?

It occurred to me that, if I were to understand not only my traveling companion who introduced me into Bayur but those who composed the resident community at any given time, I would have to start asking a different sort of question. I would have to find some more direct way to focus on the distinctive and organizing aspects of Minang cultural experience. I needed to return to my original and general question: What did the world, after all, look like to the Minangkabau—in particular, to the Minangkabau of Bayur? Unless I could focus on this question, I feared I would simply be awash in cultural details of uncertain significance. I decided to think more about what cues the Minang may have been giving me as to what was important to them.

I reread my field notes; I thought more about the range of topics the Minang had been discussing with me without my direct prompting. It occurred to me that during this time when I was wondering what sort of society, composed of what sort of persons, I had plunged into, my hosts might very likely have been wondering about me and my society. It then struck me as one of the minor ironies of anthropological fieldwork that some of the potentially most instructive events are likely to take place very early in the fieldwork when the anthropologist is least able to record or understand them. And although I did not understand much of what the Minang had been saying to each other about me, I did begin to think more about the kinds of questions they were actually asking me.

These questions had proved remarkably standardized and were the same ones that Europeans elsewhere in West Sumatra were asked and that I was asked throughout my fieldwork when meeting Minang for the first time. The initial questions, asked in no particular order, concerned my marital status, age and religion. Very often these questions were followed by two others: Did I plan to go on the local pig hunt and—since they had heard about Western

I was still fundamentally unclear about the nature of their culture.

hippies and occasionally encountered them as local tourists—what did I think of the "heepy?"

In trying to interpret these questions, I realized that the Minang were giving me a fair hearing. They did seem impressed that I had come bearing appropriate official documents from both national and regional levels of the Indonesian government, and they took seriously the fact that some of these documents specifically called on Bayur to give me its cooperation. I was convinced as well that my companion who had introduced me into town was well regarded. Furthermore, I was from the United States, and the Minang emphatically approved of my country's active anticommunist policy in Southeast Asia, regarding this as a defense of religious values. The questions the Minang asked in the face of these credentials were challenging but, I concluded, in no way hostile. It seemed likely that they were efforts to find out whether I might be accepted, even if only provisionally, into the Bayur community.

I began to inquire of my informants why they asked these questions and why they seemed to find my answers acceptable. Although fairly young, they said, I had once, at least, accepted the constraint of marriage; although fairly young and from the West, I was not a hippy—I had come to Sumatra not just to wander around indulging myself but for the serious purpose of doing research. They were reassured as well, I gathered, by the fact that although I was not a Muslim, I did as a (professed) Christian have a scriptural religion as a guide to conduct. Finally, even though I recognized that by their standards of male conduct I was quiet and certainly tentative, they had interpreted my interest in the pig hunt as showing a sufficient masculine vitality.

I began to form the impression, which became clearer with later research, that they were preoccupied in this initial inquiry by whether I would be willing or able to accept the constraints of their social life. It also became clear to me, as I contemplated these and other statements of their concern, that they must also feel I had a great deal to learn about the specific forms of their constraints if I were to fit in even in a limited way. The lessons, I realized somewhat belatedly, had begun immediately. The only criticism which the Minang made explicit to me during this early period was that I was severely deficient in the etiquette of eating and drinking in public. I was sure that my other deficiencies in etiquette had been promptly noted when I discovered that my first field notes were filled with volunteered references to good manners—*baso basi*.

I was indeed puzzled. I did not immediately see why the Minang should so emphasize that I must offer my beverage to all those present in the coffee shop before I began to eat and should so stress that I (even as a nonsmoker) must carry cigarettes so that I could offer them around whenever I sat down in a group. All of this and much more—including terms of address, ways of sitting, standing, kneeling, coming and going, consuming and serving food—was presented to me as baso basi. And while I thought I should indeed follow these forms, these local customs, I did not for some time understand why baso basi was both so pervasive and so obligatory—obligatory even to the extent that a man was required regularly to appear in public in order to demonstrate his conformity to the standards of baso basi. Because I was accustomed to measuring individual worth primarily in terms of a personal self, I did not for some time understand why the Minangkabau were accustomed to measuring individual worth primarily in terms of the extent to which an individual observed baso basi. To me, and I think to most contemporary Americans, the Minangkabau view that manners make the person seemed comparable to and about as remote as the statement made in 1687 by a Virginian gentleman that his children had "better be never born than ill-bred" (cited in Schlesinger 1946). I did, however, persevere in learning local etiquette once I realized that I would not be regarded as even an honorary member of the community until I conformed to this set of constraints.

After I demonstrated that I was willing to accept the basic socialization of learning baso basi, I noted that the older men in particular began stuffing me with information about other Minang customs, other aspects of *adaik* (*adat*). Minang adaik subsumes all that is right and proper in indigenous Minang society. (A distinction is frequently made by the Minang between adaik and Islam, since the latter was not accepted by the Minang until the sixteenth century and the relationship between them is formulated in various ways. The most common statement of the current relationship is that adaik is ultimately subject to correction by Islam, although adaik in its present form is seen as requiring little or no such correction. It is, moreover, an important part of adaik to give strong support to Islam.)

My initial reaction to the Minang emphasis on presenting and explaining adaik was very different from my initial reaction to their emphasis on the importance of baso basi. Rather than mild frustration and perplexity, I felt delight. I was not, then, to be disappointed in my original hope that the Minang could provide an explicit interpretation of major aspects of their cultural behavior. However, I was soon disconcerted to realize that *nothing* in adaik is without meaning. The four towers of the village mosque, it was volunteered, stood for the four groups in the village; the intrusion of a pillar supporting a house beam within a ceremonial space stood for the role of the lineage leader who gives support to his followers; the number of sides of a ceremonial packet of betel mixture stood for the various types of speech—or, depending on my informant, for the number of ingredients in the mixture, or for the number of rulers in Minangkabau history, and so on. Although many of these interpretations were obviously improvised on the spot, each was delivered with certainty as a fully valid explanation. And in those relatively few cases in which an interpretation could not be produced, I was assured that the particular bit of adaik under discussion did have a meaning and that there was someone who knew precisely what that meaning was.

Just as the Minang expectations differed from mine concerning the relative importance of manners—baso basi—in an individual's conduct, so, too, I came to discover, did their expectations differ from mine concerning what constituted an adequate explanation of adaik. Although the Minang did provide explicit interpretations of their cultural behavior—and in fact took considerable pride in being able to do so—these explanations were from my perspective much too shallow to be convincing. They seemed shallow because they appeared so prolific, facile, ad hoc, and dogmatic, and because they focused on what were in my view the superficialities of overt form. That they found their expectations reasonable concerning the central importance of baso basi in personal conduct and I did not, and that they found their interpretations of adaik fully satisfactory and I did not, at least implies that the Minang and I were following different assumptions about the nature of proper conduct and the nature of explanation.

Since part of my initial perception that the Minangkabau premises about reality were substantially non-Western resulted from the incongruity I sensed between their expectations and mine about the nature of explanation, I must mention that I have tried to take into consideration noncultural factors which could have contributed to this impression of incongruity. As an outsider, I might have found their explanations less complete than they were because I might well have missed much that was, for the Minang, implicit or common knowledge. As an academic, I might well have expected that an explanation should systematize and show pattern to a greater extent than would be important to most of the Minang who, after all, were largely just concerned with trying to lead satisfactory lives. Both sorts of differences could lead to my greater concern with explicit coherency, comprehensiveness, and depth of interpretation. However, even after I became much less an outsider and commanded much more implicit and common knowledge than I had originally, Minang and Western standards of explanation still remained disparate. I also discovered that the explanations given by those indigenous Minang intellectuals who had carefully tended reputations as experts on their own society followed the same form, as I will later show, as the explanations given by Minang individuals with no reputation for expert knowledge or skill in explanation.

At this point in my research, I began to sense that I had found an appropriate focus. That the Minang so emphasized baso basi and the interpretation of adaik suggested that these constituted fundamental aspects of their culture. Moreover, these cultural preoccupations suggested, by their very unfamiliarity to me, ways in which I would be able to begin to understand Minang culture as indeed embodying a distinctive perspective, a distinctive view of the world. That such a distinctive perspective existed was apparent in the fact that they and I both were, of course, quite aware that they were Minang and I was not.

I thought that by examining their emphasis on baso basi as a set of social forms of obligatory importance I would be able to discern Minangkabau concepts about the nature of social form in general. This would give me access to their Minangkabau context of thought by which they understood their social forms in particular. I would then be able to understand better the many details of their life—the tense punctilious behavior of the men, the tenuous position of the grandmother's husband, as well as the many other specific facets of their cultural behavior which I had already observed or knew I would eventually encounter. My concern in understanding the Minangkabau became less in examining the multitude of particular ethnographic features which comprise Minangkabau social forms than in understanding the Minangkabau concept of social form itself.

Moreover, by examining the way in which they interpreted their lives as Minang I could further understand why they found it so important to live *as* Minang. This could help me address as a central question how they have been able to preserve at home and abroad such a vital and persistent sense of what it is to be a Minangkabau. It would help me to comprehend how the people of Bayur were still able to follow the traditional Minang ideal of selecting and modifying the influences from the wider world so that the community could continue to move with that world while remaining true to Minangkabau culture in general and village custom in particular. Understanding the Minang interpretation of themselves as Minang would also help me better understand the experiences of my companion as he visited his home village with me: how both he and the citizens of Bayur remain able to be cosmopolitan in a provincial sort of way. And I could better understand the kind of response the village of Bayur now has to the outside world. I could, in short, understand why the Minang everywhere—certainly in Bayur—still experience their strongest ties to place and person with their home villages and those there even though the attractions of the outside world are very strong and the misgivings about the limitations of village life are real. (Naim's excellent 1973 analysis of the Minang experience of living abroad extensively documents this point.)

My most general objective in my Minangkabau research and in this book has followed from my early sense that to understand the Minang was to understand their preoccupations with baso basi and the interpretation of adaik. In the discussion of the Minangkabau concept of social form and its interpretation which follows, I shall be addressing the very general question of how meaning is created, expressed, and maintained within a particular social context. Thus my analysis is intended to clarify the relationship between the way people conduct their lives and how they construct their consciousness.

PART I
THEORETICAL OVERVIEW

Chapter One
Culture as Text

Clifford Geertz concludes a recent essay by proposing that cultures should be regarded as ensembles of texts and that anthropologists should struggle to read these texts, looking over the shoulders of those whose texts they are reading (Geertz 1973, "Deep Play: Notes on the Balinese Cockfight"). He suggests that just as the Balinese cockfight is a text that the Balinese read to understand their own experience better, so too is *Macbeth* a text that members of our culture read to understand our own experience better. The basic assumption underlying this argument is that a fundamental characteristic of humans is to seek meaning, and that culture is a system of meaning. Culture in this view provides conceptual order by furnishing the concepts about social, physical, and spiritual reality which enable individuals to interpret and thus comprehend their experience. In the absence of a culturally given system of conceptual order, humans would be beset with profound confusion and consequent anxiety that would leave them incapable of effective thought or action. This assumption, probably articulated most persuasively, again, by Geertz (see Geertz 1973, "Religion as a Cultural System," in particular), can be regarded as the justification for symbolic anthropology, an anthropology which has as a primary objective the understanding of cultural views of reality and the understanding of the process by which these views are employed to render life intelligible. This process of interpreting experience—of reading texts—both follows and sustains the cultural system of meaning.

When Geertz suggests that *Macbeth* is a Western analogue to a Balinese cockfight, the question should be asked whether each text

would be read in the same way. Presumably the experience of a
Balinese attending a cockfight where he is packed together with
his fellow villagers and may be impaled by a spur or spattered with
rooster gore would be rather different from the experience of a
Westerner attending even the most compelling theater performance
of *Macbeth*. The difference between a Balinese cockfight and *Macbeth* is not just that each has a different subject but that each
subject is designed to be understood in a different manner. The
way in which a text is constructed and consequently read—the
very process of creating intelligibility itself—seems very different
in these two cases.

It is, in my view, important to explore the nature of differences
in this process of creating intelligibility. If symbolic anthropologists
wish to understand the meaning that members of a culture derive
from their texts, they need to understand the process of interpretation itself: the process of reaching an understanding is very likely
to affect what is understood. In particular, I will examine how the
way in which the Minangkabau interpret their texts of baso basi
and adaik—as well as those of the pig hunt and the ritual of
ascension to a lineage title—affects what conclusions they draw
from them about themselves, about their own culture. I will in this
be attempting to demonstrate that the way in which a cultural text
is read is itself part of a culture, that a culture contains directions
for its own understanding.

The process of creating intelligibility for any culture necessarily
reflects that culture's epistemology. Epistemologies are rarely held
in consciously articulated form but usually appear as expectations
of what is plausible and what is not, as a sense of what is reasonable
or likely, given the way that the world is thought to be. I think
that these expectations can be regarded as a kind of aesthetic
because they appear as a sense of form—a sense of what goes
together, what fits, what is congruent with reality. If different cultures can be characterized as having different views of reality and
hence different epistemologies, then cultures can also be regarded
as having distinctive aesthetics of interpretation—distinctive styles
of interpretation. The disparity I sensed between the way I interpreted etiquette and custom and the way the Minangkabau interpreted baso basi and adaik was an indication of differences between

cultural styles of interpretation. What sounded right for them did not sound right for me. Indeed, at first I had difficulty recognizing that the statement mentioned earlier—that the four towers of the village mosque stood for the four groups in the village—was even intended to be an interpretation, an explanation, in itself. What they said did not sufficiently resemble the form I expected an interpretation should take for me to accord it even potential plausibility. I kept waiting for them to get to the point, to tell me what the underlying connection was between the mosque towers and village groups that they should be thought to resemble each other. Their explanation seemed to me to be a mere introduction—the setting up of a problem rather than the solution to one. Conversely, for them their reading was by its very form regarded as potentially meaningful.

If cultures can, as I am arguing here, be distinguished by their interpretive styles, two significant implications follow.

The first implication is that this aesthetic sense substantially pervades a particular culture so that members of that culture tend to interpret their experience of persons in the same sort of way as they interpret their experience of their society more generally. Freud and Marx, to introduce examples which will be amplified later, represent and perhaps epitomize a single and largely dominant Western style for the interpretation of persons and society. Their interpretations show a similar aesthetic, since the theory of each finds meaning in roughly the same way and roughly the same location: each at a considerable remove from appearance, from reality as actually experienced. Conversely, Minangkabau, whether recognized locally as expert in the interpretation of adaik or not, present interpretations both of persons and of social forms which find meaning in each case to be very close to the actual, tangible, literal experience itself: persons are interpreted as having worth in terms of such evident characteristics as the degree to which they conform to the overt and public standards of etiquette; social forms are interpreted as having significance in terms of such evident characteristics as the number of towers of the village mosque. In both cases their interpretations struck me as similarly shallow and insufficient to reveal or approximate truth. Not only does my reaction suggest that I was responding with a Western aesthetic, based on a Western epistemology, but that both we in the West and they tend to apply a single if different aesthetic of interpretation to the various aspects of experience.

The second implication concerns a subtle form of ethnocentrism. In its most general sense, ethnocentrism refers to the process of understanding another culture in terms of the premises of one's own culture, rather than understanding that other culture in terms of its own premises. Concern in anthropology with ethnocentrism is of long standing, but what constitutes avoidable ethnocentrism remains a vital and progressively more elusive issue. This concern in its more modern form focuses less on the differences which may exist between cultures with respect to particular customs, ideas, or categories of ideas and more on the differences which may exist between cultures with respect to the basic assumptions which generate those customs, ideas, and categories of ideas. And only rather recently have anthropologists begun to make careful appraisal of the fundamental degree to which the assumptions implicit in their own, usually Western, world view may impede their efforts to perceive an alien set of cultural assumptions.

An example of this more recent kind of self-reflective concern is Anderson's essay on the Javanese concept of power (Anderson 1972). Although not himself an anthropologist, Anderson speaks to a contemporary anthropological audience when he argues that the most appropriate way to understand Javanese politics is to focus on their fundamental concept of power; and at the same time he demonstrates how Javanese politics would be fundamentally misunderstood if examined, as has often been the case, according to Western assumptions about the nature of power. A current debate concerning the degree of coherence which in fact exists in New Guinea religions is at least in part another example of the continuing anthropological recognition of the persistence in subtle form of ethnocentrism—in this case a bias stemming from Western assumptions about the nature of belief systems. (See Brunton 1980a and ensuing correspondence by Jullierat 1980, Brunton 1980b, Gell 1980, Jorgenson 1981, Johnson 1981.)

These examples for the most part concern rather specific areas of possible bias which would lead to a misreading of the particulars of non-Western cultures. I am, however, suggesting that a more fundamental bias may exist: that the most fundamental explanatory concepts of symbolic anthropology may carry a bias which would lead to a misreading of an entire body of cultural material, to a misreading of the culture itself. This bias stems from a Western aesthetic which equates adequacy of interpretation with depth of interpretation. It seems to me that the very concept of symbol itself, the essential analytic tool of symbolic anthropology, incorporates a distinctively Western view of reality, which if used incautiously as a fundamental tool of analysis, can itself introduce considerable bias. Symbols, whether in the hands of psychoanalysts, literary critics, or anthropologists, are usually regarded as having their referents—and hence their meaning—well beneath the surface, whether of a dream, a literary work, or a cultural performance. Symbols are regarded as vehicles which lead away from (mere) appearance into the more significant reality of the unapparent, where pattern and meaning are thought to reside. Turner, for instance, in expressing the concept of symbol most generally held by anthropologists, cites Jung's definition with approval: "A symbol is always the best possible expression of a relatively *unknown* fact" (Turner 1967, p. 26, original emphasis). And, again, when translating an Ndembu term, Turner (1967, p. 48) states: "A symbol, then, is a blaze or landmark, something that connects the unknown with the known."

The concept of symbol, thus, focuses attention on the concealed, the unknown, the shielded: it focuses attention on the depths, not the surfaces—not overt forms themselves. So the concept of symbol encourages anthropologists to look for meaning where, for the Minang at least, meaning does not primarily reside. Moreover, it also encourages anthropologists to distort through overinterpretation. It is always difficult to know at what point any particular interpretation—anthropological or otherwise—has proceeded far enough. Generally, Western interpretation stops only when it runs out of intellectual impetus and/or when an explanation which satisfies the Western aesthetic—a deep and coherent explanation—has been reached. Because the concept of symbol focuses attention where meaning and system may in fact not exist, and because it often does not take adequate cognizance of indigenous standards of explanation, the anthropologist may often ignore or misread those cues available from the culture under interpretation which might indicate when enough has been said.

Such cues may be particularly difficult for Western anthropologists to recognize in cultures which distinguish among their members according to either the kind or the extent of their knowledge. Individuals in New Guinea may, for instance, acquire prestige through their knowledge of esoteric ritual secrets; individuals among the Minangkabau may acquire it through their knowledge of the esoteric details of adaik. However, because individuals may acquire social distinction either through the quality or the quantity of their knowledge does not in itself mean that their knowledge is significantly different in kind from common knowledge. Only a few Karavarans (Errington 1974), for instance, know the ritual secrets necessary to construct their most important ritual figure. These secrets, however, consist of the names of particular spirits and are qualitatively the same as the knowledge everyone has about other spirits. Elsewhere in New Guinea a culture may have a set of myths or forms of a myth which men learn in sequence as they pass through the series of ritual grades. In this case, each version may simply replace another, and no version, including the most esoteric, is appreciably more opaque in meaning than any other. Comparably, among the Minang, experts know more about adaik than others, yet their understanding and their interpretations of adaik are, as I will show, conceptually equivalent to the understanding and the interpretations of the less informed. In these various instances, the knowledge of the restricted few may be in essential quality no more elusive, subtle, or generalizing than the knowledge of the multitude.

In contrast to the Western concept of symbol is the concept of sign. Signs tend to be given a rather second-rate intellectual status in Western thought. Signs require little interpretation, and certainly not deep interpretation; their meaning lies much too near the surface—much too near the apparent form itself—to offer much challenge to the interpreter or to convey information that is not too obvious to be of much interest. Turner, again, expressing the concept of sign most generally held by anthropologists, cites Jung, that "a sign is an analogous or abbreviated expression of a *known* thing" (Turner 1967, p. 26, original emphasis). Signs are thus a readily understood way of presenting that which is largely apparent.

Although both sign and symbol are, of course, Western concepts, I argue that when members of Western culture are looking for meaning—for *significant* pattern and *adequate* understanding—they tend to look for it in the form of a symbol. The most convincing explanation in Western culture, when explanations are given at all, is usually one that shows things are not as they appear. To penetrate appearance, to find underlying and comprehensive meaning, is to interpret by means of symbols. Explanation in terms of symbols conforms more closely than does explanation in terms of signs—in terms of the readily apparent—to the Western sense of how things really are. This is, again, not to deny that signs and literal interpretations are part of Western culture, nor to deny that members of Western culture may act in a preoccupied way, without giving much thought to the meaning of their actions.

Nor is this to deny that particular kinds of deep interpretations may be rejected by given Western audiences. Although the theories of Freud and Marx may conform in their structure to the Western models of interpretations, what these theories may say about particular, or even general, characteristics of human behavior may be regarded as highly objectionable. Few enthusiasts of football, for instance, welcomed Dundes's essay (1980) which offered a psychoanalytic interpretation purporting to demonstrate that homosexual themes are expressed in this sport. Nonetheless, I have found that when I discuss football in the first session of my introductory anthropology classes—without referring to this essay—students readily volunteer interpretations which have a similar structure, which in similar fashion strive for depth and comprehensiveness. They suggest that football is a kind of mock warfare and trace out the nature of and reasons for the parallel between real and mock warfare with interest and competence.

In contrast to the Western sense that meaning in its most convincing form is most likely to be found through the interpretation of symbols is the Minangkabau sense that meaning, at least meaning which can be verbally expressed, is predictably to be found through the interpretation of signs. Each culture, then, characteristically finds meaning in most convincing form at a substantially different place on the continuum between the apparent and the unapparent. (This distinction is relative rather than absolute: some signs may veer more toward the unapparent than others; some symbols may veer more toward the apparent than others.) Westerners I thus characterize as having a symbol-oriented aesthetic—a "deep" interpretation rings true to them; Minangkabau I characterize as having a sign-oriented aesthetic—a "shallow" interpretation rings true to them.[1]

How persons are to be understood and how social form—custom—is to be understood are, then, epistemological questions. These particular questions, however, are asked within a culture not only to impose meaning on experience but to address the problem of how members of that culture are to live together in relative concord. The concern of symbolic anthropology in understanding the way in which a culture establishes a conceptual order can appropriately be allied with the more traditional anthropological interest in understanding the way in which a culture establishes social order. Demonstrated perhaps most notably by Turner's writings on the Ndembu (e.g., Turner 1967) was the postwar recognition by social anthropologists that, even in tribal societies, social order, however maintained, was not maintained easily. Thus, if humans need to make their life in general intelligible to themselves, surely a major concern must be to make the nature and basis of their collective life in particular intelligible to themselves. Intellectual concerns are focused by pragmatic concerns.

Of the sign-oriented texts which the Minangkabau use to "orient themselves in a world otherwise opaque" (Geertz 1973, p. 363), those which are of most interest to me are indeed those which bear most directly on the nature of their social life. The two related

1. I recognize that *symbol* and *sign* are not always defined as Jung, Turner, and I are here defining them. Particularly in contexts in which anthropologists, linguists, and others are referring simply to the fact that one thing may represent another, then it may be convenient to use either term to encompass the other. Turner himself, for instance, sometimes uses this more inclusive definition of *symbol*. However, when he wishes to make the distinction between relatively unapparent and relatively apparent, he presents this as the distinction between *symbol* and *sign* (Turner 1967, page 29). This latter usage is, in my view, the more common—and the more appropriate.

texts I have selected for my major focus are those two activities
which first attracted my attention because they so preoccupy the
Minangkabau themselves: the activity of embodying baso basi and
the activity of interpreting adaik.

Some of the problems of understanding and achieving their particular social order which the Minangkabau confront in these two
major texts are problems common to most, if not all, complex
societies. One major problem concerns how to determine the appropriate relationship between individual constraint and freedom.
This involves determining the degree of diversity of personal experience that can be permitted within a society. A second and
related general problem concerns how to determine the appropriate
relationship between social continuity and change.

These, then, are the problems which the Minangkabau confront,
and if they are general, perhaps universal, problems in complex
societies, the Minangkabau solutions to them are rather distinctive.
Moreover, while the general subject of the Minangkabau texts may
be similar to the general subject of our important Western texts,
the way in which their texts garner and yield meaning is, I have
suggested, substantially dissimilar to the way ours garner and yield
meaning. If I am correct in arguing that the Minangkabau express
a sign-oriented aesthetic in their interpretations of baso basi and
adaik, how does this interpretive style relate to what they are
actually saying about their social order: what does the form of the
Minangkabau commentary on these subjects have to do with what
they are trying to say about them? What, in other words, is the
link between a message *conveyed* by signs and a message *about*
the way that freedom and constraint, continuity and change can
be balanced in a Minangkabau community? These questions speak
to my most general interest in the relationship of thought—its shape
and its content—and the social order: in the relationship of meaning
and social context.

The Minangkabau orientation toward signs does enable them to
deal rather neatly with these general problems of complex societies
as they manifest themselves with increasing force in the particular
Minangkabau setting. The Minangkabau have in fact confronted
these problems in acute form for centuries. Their culture manifests
itself in small, proudly distinctive, independent villages which have

for generations sent young men abroad to gain experience—that is, to be seasoned, broadened, and disciplined by the larger world. Their culture also holds a concept of person that regards individuals as unreliable because they are so actively self-interested. Minang believe that if the self-interest of individuals went unchecked, social form would disappear and social order would be impossible. Hence it is essential that society exercise control. Total control of individuals, however, is neither possible in Minangkabau social theory nor in their experience, in part because Minang regard individuals as extremely adept at concealing their motives. Significantly, the Minang, although shrewd and often cynical about human motivation in general, have little interest in or capacity for understanding why particular individuals are the way they are.

Because the Minang believe that individuals are unreliable and strongly motivated by self-interest, and because they cannot identify with certainty those individuals who might be exceptions to that general view of human nature, they demand that all individuals continually demonstrate their willingness to conform to basic Minang standards of order. Social control appears in the demands by the local community, the *masyarakat*, that it receives frequent evidence of outward conformity to adaik—frequent *signs* in the form of etiquette, baso basi, that energetic self-interest is being constrained. The effectiveness of this form of control is substantially limited to the public realm and is, moreover, even there further limited in the case of young men—referred to simply as "youth."

Minang recognize that this youth cannot be disciplined effectively, that they cannot be trusted with other people's belongings, and that they in fact do not display more than elementary and sporadic baso basi. Encouraging youth to go abroad is explicitly regarded by the Minang as clearly desirable, in part because they then pass through the most obstreperous period of their lives creating trouble for someone else and are disciplined by the necessity of making their own living far from home. Once back from abroad, these young men are able to show the signs of their newly accepted discipline by conforming along with the rest of the community to baso basi, irrespective of any diversity of predilection and habit which might have been acquired through diversity of experience abroad. In this way, all are eventually brought under sufficient control by the local community so that social order is possible.

Although diversity of experience gives no individual an exemption from the requirements of baso basi, this diversity is nonetheless acknowledged and valued in other ways. The local Minang community feels that it would stagnate, not move with the times or fulfill its potential for development (see Abdullah 1971, 1972, and Mrazek 1972) unless it were continually exposed to the new experiences acquired by its young men while abroad. However, any proposed change in traditional practices which might be suggested by these experiences must be closely scrutinized by the community so that it can preserve its distinctively Minang cultural integrity.

The Minang thus balance continuity and change through decisions made by the local community which specify what sorts of change are both possible and desirable. The community is able to solve this general social and conceptual problem in part through distinguishing between the peripheral and the core elements of adaik. The peripheral elements can usually be allowed to change as long as the core elements remain fundamentally the same. For instance, when a man ascends to his matrilineage title, he is treated with extreme respect and pledges to look after his fellow lineage members. The particular forms of respect he receives in this ceremony are susceptible to change, as are his particular duties in looking after his lineage members; conversely, the central—and for the Minang, entirely evident—idea that a titleholder receives respect and accepts responsibility is not regarded as susceptible to change. The distinction between peripheral and core elements of adaik is achieved in substantial measure through the continual process of interpreting adaik. (The distinction between peripheral and core elements is *not* the distinction between sign and symbol, since the meaning of both peripheral and core is fully recognized.)

The Minangkabau balance continuity and change within adaik in this way by using signs in interpreting and discussing adaik. Many of the particular forms of adaik are regarded as signs, or illustrations, of the core elements of adaik. In this way, these core elements which comprise adaik's fundamental truths can be regarded as receiving appropriate expression in a variety of specific practices. These specific practices can be recognized as subject to change over time, but despite these changes they remain acceptable to the Minangkabau because they are still signs pointing to the central truths of adaik. Thus, when a custom changes it can often be regarded as still providing a valid illustration of a fundamental and inviolable, yet clearly recognized, element of Minangkabau adaik.

The sign-oriented aesthetic does not lend itself to a rethinking of the basis of culture itself. By focusing, for example, on the different ways in which respect for a clan titleholder may be exhibited, the potentially radical and perplexing question of why a clan holder should receive respect—or even why respect should be an essential part of the social order—never arises. Signs thus help the Minang understand and accept social changes by regarding those changes as mere variant forms of expression of invariant—core—elements of adaik. Because signs refer to that which is clearly recognized and unassailably given, they provide for the Minang a relatively convenient, economical, and conservative way to deal with basic and common problems concerning social order and social change—problems exacerbated by the recent increase in pressure from the outside world.

By utilizing signs as the everyday currency of meaning and by asserting and demonstrating that everything has meaning, the Minangkabau can continue to feel that their life is supremely reasonable, that baso basi is not mere constraint and that adaik and its interpretation are not mere convention and opinion—in other words, that morality is reality and aesthetics is ethics. If morality is an aspect of reality, social constraint—constraint of persons—is not viewed as arbitrary, as mere constraint or convention, or even simply as socially desirable. Rather, it is viewed as entirely reasonable. If aesthetics is equivalent to ethics, the essentially aesthetic judgment of conduct on which social constraint is based is not experienced as only opinion or as mere preference, but again rings true as entirely reasonable. When morality and reality, aesthetics and ethics are viewed and experienced as being inseparable, then social life itself and the judgments and interpretations on which it is based are viewed and experienced as supremely right and proper.

Such an accord has become very elusive in our own culture.

Among contemporary Americans there is simply not the unquestioning and general acceptance of a set of values that would make signs plausible for the construction and reading of texts. Diversity based on region, ethnicity, class, race, gender, and generation assail the sense of cultural certainty of even those who consider their values to be quintessentially American. Most of us must, at least in the process of socializing our children, attempt to render plausible our basic beliefs. This effort stems from the realization of parents and their children that parental views on such topics as religion, the importance of regular hours, appropriate modes of discipline or reward, and the value of family life itself may not be universally shared, not even by immediate neighbors. Moreover, parents are aware that their views on a host of social issues such as abortion, the death penalty, working wives, to name a few, are not universally shared. They may find themselves in discussion with children or with other adults trying to justify their particular perspective. In the face of a skeptical audience they may have to trace out a train of interconnected consequences to support their positions. Indeed, they may be forced to provide "reasons" for their "reasons" and not infrequently in so doing realize just how hard it is to convince others that their personal philosophy really should provide the basis for a particular set of social forms.

The major question implicit in all of this discussion of the Minang and their use of signs is whether the Minangkabau ever portray a level of experience that cannot be elucidated by signs. Do Minangkabau signs rest on symbols, on efforts to depict an unapparent, fundamentally illusive, reality?

The "really real," of course, is difficult for any culture actually to specify. The closest the Minang get in their adaik to making such profound statements about themselves comes with two sorts of enactments: in the ascension of a man to the panghulu title of his lineage and in the pig hunt. The panghulu ascension is an ordering—an enactment of maximal constraint, barely energized control, and scrupulous observance of social form. The pig hunt is not an ordering. It is an enactment of barely controlled energy. The intersecting analytic themes of freedom and constraint, continuity and change, appear in these particularly dense texts—master texts—as preoccupations with the nature of social form and of energy. The panghulu ascension embodies ideas of constraint and continuity of pattern and order which allow a Minangkabau village to maintain its valued distinctiveness and proximity to truth. The pig hunt embodies the ideas of energy and force which allow a Minangkabau village to remain vital. Individuals must be granted sufficient freedom so that their energy and force can appear as the initiative and drive necessary, not only for there to be social action within the village, but for the village to change with the times and for individual Minangkabau to exert a significant influence in the larger world that will bring credit to the home village and the Minangkabau culture itself.

As I will show, however, these enactments, despite their length, complexity, and their binding up of the participants into the activity itself, are nevertheless interpreted by the Minangkabau as being composed of signs, comprising well-known and well-accepted indications about the nature of social life. To the extent, though, that the panghulu ascension and the pig hunt are regarded as integrated and consistently patterned activities, they can be experienced by the Minangkabau as reference points of quintessential adaik and of quintessential vitality, namely, as providing the most undiluted experiences available to the Minangkabau of what they recognize social forms and persons actually to be.

I have here set out the intellectual context in which I am working and have provided an introduction to my argument. The elaboration and substantiation of that argument make up the rest of the book. In Part 2, I begin my close interpretation of the Minangkabau by addressing in detail the question, thus far only introduced, of why they so greatly value etiquette. I will then further examine the Minangkabau concept of person, community, and social order. In Part 3, I further examine the question of why the Minangkabau interpret their customs so extensively. At this point, I will examine their concept of truth and understanding as it is embedded in their concept of the community, the nature of communal discussion, and the role of the expert on adaik within the community. Parts 2 and 3 thus concern conduct, and the understanding of that conduct, in everyday life.

In Part 4 I examine Minangkabau efforts to place everyday life itself in perspective. In the ritual of ascension to the panghulu title of a lineage and in the frenzy of the pig hunt, the Minangkabau act in ways that they regard as extraordinary—ways that are not part of everyday life but are experienced as paradigmatic of everyday life. Finally, I will present my conclusions about the Minangkabau and emphasize further the idea that each culture has a favored aesthetic judgment so that the interpretations of persons and social forms follow a similar pattern. I will then also discuss briefly possible reasons for such difference in interpretive styles as they pertain to differences in social context.

PART II
BASO BASI AND THE BASIS OF SOCIAL ORDER

Chapter Two
The Concept of Person

Perhaps the most salient characteristic the Minangkabau see in themselves, and the one most frequently stressed to the foreign visitor, is that they are not straightforward, *terus terang*. Their view of themselves as oblique rests on a concept of persons in which individuals are ambivalently regarded as having not only a fundamentally disruptive and selfish nature but also the capacity to conceal that nature for good or ill: refinement conceals it by actually accepting social constraint; deviousness, by only pretending to accept social constraint. Refinement can thus lead to social order and, I suspect for these Muslims, to personal religious salvation; deviousness, in turn, can lead to social anarchy and to personal religious damnation.

One highly valued manifestation of being oblique is traditional formal speech, larded with archaic Minangkabau and packed with the set allusions, metaphors, and aphorisms which characterize the highly controlled language of ritual. All public occasions, whether a commemorative prayer, a wedding, or a visit by civil administrators, begin with the host displaying as much of this refined speech as he knows. He expresses the boundless extent of his pleasure that the guests honor him with their presence; he expresses the extreme importance of this kind of occasion as an essential part of Minangkabau adaik. The guests, often through an impromptu spokesman, respond by indicating how great their pleasure is in listening to the words, sweet as coconut cream, of their host. In this context, and in the very pervasive realm of Minang baso basi generally, concealment of private motives and objectives is socially commendable and is in fact essential if there is to be social order. But concealing motives may also be used to evade public scrutiny and undermine social order. It is this second aspect of being impenetrably oblique that creates among the Minang a fundamental uncertainty about what anyone is really up to.

As a newly arrived foreigner, I was often warned by the Minang themselves not to believe automatically what anyone said. As one man told me, two and two may equal four in America, but not necessarily among the Minangkabau. Ironically, at the very moment he told me this he was confirming the wisdom of his statement: posing as someone only concerned with my best interests, he was in the process of unfairly maligning my assistant, claiming that I should not trust him so that he, I was quite sure, could replace him in my employ. This disjunction between real and apparent motives is reflected in the traditional saying which advises one to preserve a calm exterior toward an enemy even though seething like a tiger inside. It can also be seen in the typical Minangkabau reaction to the Muslim custom, on Hari Raya at the end of the month of fasting, of asking forgiveness from those of the community who might have been offended during the previous year. At this time one stresses sincerity by asking pardon from the inside as well as from the outside. Such a statement may facilitate the resumption of normal social relationships but is rarely believed as indicating any real change of disposition.

Minang display considerable perception about human motivation. For instance, my landlady gave me a very expensive gift of a hand-embroidered bedspread, which she asked me to take home to my mother. My assistant, who had witnessed the presentation of this gift, and I spent much time speculating about it: was it simply the manifestation of good will—which he very much doubted? did she give it to me perhaps because I reminded her of the son she had never had? or was it an indirect marriage proposal? He thought that the last possibility was most likely, especially as the gift was ultimately destined for my mother: whatever the inclinations of the prospective couple, he said, a marriage could take place only if the respective mothers agreed. If it were a marriage proposal, we wondered who was being proposed as the bride. My landlady was divorced but was some ten years older than I; her oldest daughter, on the other hand, was only fifteen, some twenty years younger than I. My assistant thought that the daughter was the more likely candidate despite our difference in years, because Minang women sometimes do marry at fifteen. We also discussed whether this entire line of interpretation was correct: should my landlady's action be interpreted purely in the Minangkabau context of meaning, or should my status as a foreigner be taken into account? Then we considered how I could avoid being coerced by having accepted this gift without alienating the donor. In these speculations thus far he seemed to follow the same lines of inquiry that we in the West would follow.

However, this and other conversations about motives did suggest differences between Minangkabau and Western views of people. My discussion with my assistant about my landlady's gift only concerned the way human beings behave in general. What our discussion lacked was specificity: we did not discuss why a particular person had behaved in a particular fashion. Why, I wondered, had my landlady chosen to act in a way that both my assistant and I regarded as inappropriate? As my thoughts turned to this question, I began to consider what I knew about her. She was, I recognized, in a rather anomalous position in the community. Better educated than most, she was a midwife and medical practitioner with a Western kind of training. Yet she was not well paid and not very prosperous. She also felt somewhat superior socially and had sought to associate with the better educated and more important people in the area. She had, for instance, invited all of the local schoolteachers to a banquet and, in honor of my visit, proposed another banquet to include the mayor, the regional civil, military, and police administrators, and some of the most respected local lineage titleholders. Such banquets in the absence of specific occasions as weddings were most unusual. Yet despite these social aspirations, she was not regarded by the community as a particularly important person. Was her latest action of giving me the gift, I wondered, simply another reflection of the same kind of frustration and insecurity that seemed to characterize her relationship to the community.

When I voiced these thoughts to my assistant, he simply shrugged in puzzled indifference. And when I then asked him why he thought my landlady had behaved inappropriately, he shrugged again. In this instance and in many others, I never encountered a Minang who was interested in constructing a picture of that complex of personal—as opposed to generally human—motivation we call character. Indeed, as I later learned, even Minangkabau novels that follow the Western model of authorial omniscience strike Western readers as being very flat in their portrayal of "character" (Phillips, personal communication). Minangkabau views and experiences of human behavior, based as they are upon a set of standard interpretations, are stereotyped.

This same stereotyped response emerged in response to my questions about local individuals who were considered to be mad (*gilo*). Many of the crazy men could easily be identified as deviant: they wore dirty, shabby, ragged, ill-fitting garments, in contrast to other Minang who were always dressed neatly in clean clothes unless they were actually engaged in heavy work such as cultivating a flooded rice field, repairing a road, or carrying bricks to a mason. Their speech, I was told, also was often inappropriate and obviously unrelated to the immediate context. Others regarded as crazy were more difficult to identify. They looked like everyone else and were regarded as entirely coherent in speech. One such man was evidently chronically depressed; another was regarded as mad, only as far as I could tell, because he was milder and less assertive, than other men. When I inquired why a particular individual had gone mad, I received potentially plausible answers but ones drawn almost at random from a cultural catalog of general reasons why people do become mad. This catalog was the same irrespective of whether the individual involved was obviously disoriented or simply not as contentious as most. Perhaps, my informants suggested, his wife had left him; he worried too much about money; his mother had died; he had failed an exam; he was ensorcelled. When I pointed out that these experiences, although unfortunate, were rather common ones and did not account for why only some individuals suffering them became mad, my point was accepted. But no matter how hard I pushed to set up comparisons of individuals who had lost their mothers but preserved their sanity with those who had lost both, I could never get an even hypothetical answer that would suggest a reason why any given individual might be particularly affected by certain sorts of experiences. Instead I simply heard reiterations that some individuals lose control ("drop the reins") and others do not. To be sure, this is the way that most of us in the West would leave such a problem if it arose casually in our daily lives, but we would, if pushed, be able to provide a more detailed answer that in some way reflected our Western concept of character.

Not surprisingly, the concept of character is also absent from the Minang view of child rearing. The Minang do see children as having attitudes and behavior formed by parental influence and feel that parents are responsible for teaching them how to live as orderly members of the community. Parents do this, in large part, by teaching them to feel shame so that they will be responsive to community pressures and exhibit baso basi. But I could elicit only the vaguest sort of explanation when I asked why a particular young man was, even relative to other Bayur young men, much too troublesome for community tastes. My informants answered my specific questions about this young man and his father readily enough. The father was much admired as an eminent religious figure, known for his learning and piety, and his success as a businessman. His son was able simply to go into his father's store in Padang and help himself to new and stylish clothing from the shelves and spending money from the till. He would then return and loiter with conspicuous insolence in his home village of Bayur, to the envy of the other youths and the extreme annoyance of the adults. Few Westerners would have had much difficulty in speculating about a particular history of interpersonal dynamics between this father and son which could have produced this young man's behavior. Indeed, popular American magazines such as *Reader's Digest* are filled with such accounts. The Minangkabau, however, responded to my inquiry of why this young man had become as he was by simply stating that, despite the influence of a fatherly paragon of religious and economic virtue, sometimes a child did not turn out well. This reason is even less specific than those given to explain why a person goes mad. The metaphor the Minang used was that of a bunch of bananas: most are good but frequently there is a bad one. And that was all they could say about this young man and his upbringing.

In their own view, then, Minangkabau are in any practical sense fundamentally inknowable: they avoid revealing their motives in speech; their actions are not in any very precise way predictable or retrospectively explicable. If they had a rosy view of human nature, such a concept of person would cause them little concern, for although individual motivation might be obscure in its particulars, it could in general be assumed to be benign and orderly in its manifestations. This, however, is not their view of human nature: they believe that if individuals were free to follow their own inclinations—if they were *bebas*, a term with very negative connotations, indicating freedom from constraint—then murder, rapine, pillage, and general mayhem would result. Even under the set of constraints on which the Minangkabau social order in fact rests there are not infrequent manifestations of disruptive self-seeking human nature in the form of vandalism, sorcery, and slander. For example, my assistant reported to me one morning, with a mixture of anger and resignation, that a magnificent clove tree belonging to his grandmother had been girdled the previous night. It had been killed for no apparent reason other than to deprive her of a tidy income. Indeed, the vandalism was timed so that she would not be able to benefit from what promised to be an unusually good harvest. He had no one in mind as a suspect—it could, he said, have been anybody. Comparably, serious or chronic illness is often regarded as stemming from the malevolence of unknown persons. Many Minang have also had the experience of trying to combat discrediting rumors about them which may suddenly circulate through the community.

Sometimes the sources of these forms of aggression are known or suspected, but often the victims respond with baffled resignation and with comments, to me at least, about the more negative aspects of community life.

Given the Minang view of human nature, coercion is essential if social forms are to persist and social order is to be possible. However, the social forms through which coercion is expressed are also shaped by this view: because of their suspicion of others, Minangkabau carefully limit situations in which any individual has direct power over them.

Because most people are regarded as potentially untrustworthy (excepting close matrilineal kin, most particularly one's mother

and siblings), an individual is likely to feel that the only person
he can trust is himself. The economic implications of this individualism have been thoroughly discussed (cf. Naim 1973): Minang
are aggressive and resourceful in running their own businesses but
find it difficult to engage in cooperative enterprises. (The self-
reliance implicit in Islam probably also contributes to the Minangkabau sense of individualism; certainly the correlation between
Islam and entrepreneurial business has been noted in the literature.
See Geertz 1968.) Not surprisingly, most businesses are small. All
of the shops in Bayur, for instance, are owned and run by a single
individual, sometimes with the help of his wife. The market, which
convenes every Friday in Bayur and every day in the regional
market town, shows enterprises of similar scale and organization.
The market consists of rows of small stalls or, in some cases,
simply adjacent areas on the ground or on the long municipally
owned tables, where the proprietor, for a small fee to the community, can display his own wares. (In fact, it often resembles an
American flea market.) Larger-scale enterprises do exist, although
they are usually still under the control of a single individual. I was
often told which of the buses running through Bayur belonged to
a particular enterprise, but this enterprise was always described
as owned by a specific man. Such a successful individual will, of
course, have a number of employees, for not every Minang has
sufficient resources to operate his own business. However, if Minang must work for other Minang in their home village, they are
careful not to place themselves in a position where that economic
relationship can become the general basis of power over them: for
instance, they are reluctant to work for a kinsman because they
wish to be free to break off an economic relationship at any time.
Furthermore, coercion of any sort within the village is limited, for
men anyway, by the ever-present cultural option of going abroad.

Commensurate with this individualism is the absence of endur-
ing factions within Bayur. Thus, when two individuals quarrel
each may seek support for his position from others throughout the
community at large rather than from some preexisting group.
Given the atomism of Minangkabau economic life, a man simply
does not have a set of economic allies or dependents to call on.
Moreover, kin ties do not automatically provide a man with a group

of supporters. Although a disputant might expect support from his
own brother, he would not necessarily expect his matrilineage to
mobilize on his behalf. Indeed, his matrilineal seniors—his mother's brother and his panghulu—probably would carefully avoid
taking sides so that they could work with their counterparts to settle
the dispute as quickly as possible in the interests of community
tranquility. Bayur is still largely endogamous, and all, irrespective
of their particular matrilineal affiliations, consider themselves
members of a single and fundamentally united community. Low-
level disputes in Bayur consequently remain disputes between particular individuals. They do not provide the occasion for economic
networks to be activated, as in New Guinea, or for kinship groups
to be mobilized, as in Africa.

The individuality that characterizes the way in which Minang
conduct their economic life and their disputes also appears in their
political interaction. Adult males, at least, interact as political
equals. To be sure, some individuals in Bayur are regarded as
more important, more respected than others (prestige is usually
based on wealth, knowledge of adaik, and knowledge of religion)
but, with two partial exceptions, these individuals are neither more
powerful nor more autonomous than others.

One partial exception is the mayor who, if he governs at all—
and, indeed, he is by no means always able to get local compliance
or cooperation for his projects—draws on the power of the central
government and relies heavily on traditional decision-making pro-
cesses. I discovered, for example, that my permission to stay in
Bayur was not the result of mayorial fiat. The authorization for my
study, which I brought with me from the bureaucratic heights of
Padang and Jakarta, required a final confirmation from the citizens
of Bayur. The mayor had first carefully sampled public opinion
before sanctioning my presence and project by finding me a permanent place to stay.

The other partial exception is the panghulu, who are installed
in office as the titleholding representatives of their matrilineages.
Each maintains order within his matrilineage and is responsible
to the other panghulu and to the village at large for the conduct
of his matrilineal kin. Panghulu[1] do have power—especially con-

---

1. Minangkabau terms have the same form in both singular and plural and are
so used in this book.

cerning the disposition of land—and are strongly enjoined by adaik to use that power for public good rather than for private advantage. Nevertheless, particularly during the Dutch administration of the early twentieth century that power was subject to abuse. Matrilineally inherited land should, according to adaik, be sold only when certain vital matrilineal needs can be met in no other way, as when the house sheltering the matrilineage will collapse unless money for immediate repair can be found from the sale of ancestral land. The panghulu's signature is required as evidence that such dire circumstances exist. During this period, panghulu were accused of providing their signatures when no emergency existed, in exchange for a major percentage of the sale (see Schrieke 1955). That even panghulu are not always trustworthy despite the constraint expected from them must serve as additional confirmation to the Minang that their rather cynical view of human nature is accurate.

Minang often talk about how difficult they are to govern, citing proverbs to the effect that if you try to lead a water buffalo (the emblem of the Minang), it will butt you, or if you try to push it, it will kick you. If the motives of all individuals, including those of potential leaders, are suspect and, moreover, if people for that and other reasons are reluctant to take orders, virtually the only manageable political system is one based on consensus, in which all are equally and mutually constrained. Among the Minang, formal and informal meetings of all sorts, including those ritual events which only panghulu attend, are characterized by attempts to reach consensus, or *mupakaik*. Consensus is regarded by the Minang as the dominant principle of their social life. It is also the dominant principle of their intellectual life, since in consensus lies not only order but truth. Only through emphasizing the importance of consensus can the tendency of individuals to pursue selfish objectives, and thus to stray from the path of traditional wisdom, be checked.

The centrality of consensus as a social and intellectual principle expresses the centrality of the community as a social group. The community is relentless in its demand for demonstrations that everyone is accepting the constraints on which social life is based—that no one is remaining aloof from, or is actively violating, those constraints. Just as the source of constraint, the community as a whole, reflects the Minangkabau concept of person, so does the scope of that constraint reflect the Minangkabau concept of person.

The required conformity to social form is both shallow and pervasive: shallow because it focuses only on outward behavior without concerning itself with the inner person, which given the Minang view of person is accessible only to Allah; pervasive because it covers all aspects of outward behavior in an apparent effort to reduce the private sector to that which is truly inaccessible. Minang society demands all that it can; but, given its view of person, its demands, although sometimes irksome, are usually rather easy to meet. Certainly in daily life the most that Minang society can hope to receive is frequent, if not continual, evidence from its members of their commitment to social order, their acceptance of constraint. Baso basi, I will argue, as the currency of constraint, forms a daily ritual in which individuals attempt to demonstrate that they are suppressing their selfish inclinations in the interests of social order rather than concealing them to evade and undermine that order.

Every evening from about 4:30 until sundown and evening prayers at about 6:30, the main street and the coffee shops are full of men strolling, sitting, chatting, arguing, regaling, and calling out to each other in passing. This daily congregation is the community, at least the male portion of it. (For women, most of the socializing is in and around their houses during the day, and at the mosque or prayer houses during the evening. They do not engage in this daily public display perhaps, in part, because they have a secure domestic sphere. The men, for reasons discussed in more detail later, do not.) By this time in the late afternoon the artisans and farmers have finished their day's work. First they bathe next to their houses in the small enclosures which straddle the little streams that are directed through the fish tanks of the community from the irrigated fields and mountain slopes above Bayur down to the lake below. Then, after a quick supper with their families and donning fresh shirts and trousers or sarongs, they venture out into the community. Those who operate the stores and shops will continue working until much later in the evening but, perhaps leaving their wives in charge, will take a few minutes to bathe and eat. They

Every evening men congregate in the coffee shops to smoke and be seen socializing.

can, in any case, take part in the evening round of sociability in their shops.

There is relaxation and camaraderie among these men, but there is also a continual testing and evaluation by each to determine the current state of his membership in the community. As the men wander up and down the street, little groups form and disperse and, as they disperse, some men may be left behind. Sometimes these men stay for a while where they are, especially if they are sitting outside of their houses which happen to border the main street, and wait for someone else to stop; sometimes they wander across the street to join another stranded householder; sometimes they stroll down the street to join another group; sometimes they just go off to pray. No one wants to be alone, or to be seen alone, because being alone suggests that there may be something wrong with his status in the community, that he may not be compatible (*cocok*). There are other situations that test whether one is fitting in: weddings, house raisings, funerals, and harvests all provide occasions for the host to watch anxiously to see whether the turnout from the community is large. Indeed, many of these events seem designed to provide the opportunity for as many people as possible to attend. One of the principal activities at a wedding, for instance, is the gathering of large numbers of men and women within a house to watch the bride and groom sit for several hours, motionless and perspiring in heavy rented finery. Some of these occasions are by invitation; at others, like funerals, everyone is welcome. But even if invitations are issued, the net is cast to include many, and the number of people who come can provide a measure of one's compatibility with the community. If the turnout is poor, reasons such as inclement weather or pressing work in the rice fields may be offered by the nervous host to those who do come.

There is nothing mystical, abstract, or elusive about the village community: it assembles in this informal way every day. My informants were explicit that the point of all this strolling and socializing of an evening is not just to test one's relationship with the community; it is also to remain on good terms with it. To subject oneself to public scrutiny and not be found wanting, while at the same time scrutinizing others, is the activity which provides the minimal and operational definition of membership in the community. Conversely, I was told that those who do not put in their time with the community in this way find themselves ostracized. If such a person falls ill, the conversation in the coffee shops will be that it does not matter if he should die; in fact, the quicker the better. If he does die, no one will stop by to help his children with the funeral. In contrast, if someone who is on good terms with the community is sick, many will come to inquire after his health or, depending on the course of the illness, help at his funeral.

Most of the evening conversation within the community is trivial, my informants conceded. Little direct information is transmitted when someone strolling down the street is asked where he is going and he replies that he is going west. Nor is it important when another person walking by is told that a few minutes ago he was walking east with two people and now he is walking west with someone else, when his reply is that such indeed was the case. But all agreed about the pleasure of receiving such salutations because it is just awfully nice to feel on good terms with the community.

These salutations, which comprise so much of the discourse

At a wedding large numbers of men and women gather to watch the
motionless and perspiring bride and groom.

within the community, are part of baso basi in its most general, least demanding form and are known even by children. They express equality between peers and the varying degrees of respect appropriate to a mother's brother, a father, or a brother-in-law. Other salutations may be directed toward the community at large, as in the coffee shop when one offers food and beverage to all present before eating or drinking oneself. (There are other forms of baso basi which are more esoteric and concern forms of ceremonial speech, seating and serving arrangements on special occasions, and so on. I shall give examples of these later, in the discussion of the ritual of ascension to a panghulu title.)

Thus, baso basi, with its prescriptions of behavior expected from members of various social categories as well as from the community generally, determines the form of much casual social interaction. To be a member of the community requires not only that there be constant social interaction—to be alone is to suggest a lack of commitment to sociality itself—but also that the social interaction be in accord with the Minangkabau understanding of what the social forms are. Observance of baso basi as the embodiment of particular social forms seems to indicate a commitment to social forms per se.

In addition to requiring continual demonstrations of baso basi, the community also closely observes conduct in general. Even the commonplace exchanges that comprise much of the daily requirement of sociability often have an inquisitorial edge. "Have you prayed yet?" is an evening pleasantry, but one which also serves as a reminder that one certainly does not want to be known as a person who does not pray regularly, who does not observe religious forms. Many, especially the young men feel constricted in the village. They regard life there as narrow and people as intolerant, especially in contrast to what they may have experienced or anticipate experiencing in some urban center while they are abroad. Perhaps one of the reasons people are regarded as opaque is that they learn to hide their thoughts from the scrutiny of the community. Certainly they learn to hide themselves physically during the Friday noon prayer if they have not attended, or from a funeral procession if they do not wish to be bothered to join it. In fact, I once teased an informant about his tendency to slip from my front porch in to my house whenever he saw a funeral procession forming. He was quick to respond by mentioning those funerals in which he had been conspicuous by volunteering to be one of the gravediggers. Clearly he did not want me or anyone else to suggest that he was insufficiently active in community affairs.

Although the community may often be regarded as constrictive, it is not thought of in any long view as unjust or capricious. Rather, the community, as suggested earlier, is in several senses regarded as a repository of truth. It is the judge of whether adaik is being properly followed or interpreted. The recognition of a particular individual as especially knowledgeable about adaik comes from the community, which finds his interpretations compatible with its own sense of what adaik is about. Moreover, there is a general respect for the community's ability to decide informally on the merits of a case when, in a quarrel between individuals, each attempts to mobilize the community on his side. (In such cases, as mentioned, the community may be divided temporarily, but not to the extent, in Bayur at least, that factions are formed.)

For instance, at one point my assistant was very troubled because an older man who coveted his job with me was openly maligning him throughout the community. (This was the same man, mentioned earlier, who had told me me not to trust my assistant.) My assistant responded to this attack by making a noticeably greater effort than usual to circulate along the main street during the evening, so that he could greet as many people as possible and demonstrate to all the extent of his sociability. He admitted to me that he was afraid the community might turn against him. In response to my question of whether he was trying to win over or mobilize any particular group within the community, he said he was not, adding that once the community at large had heard his story, it would support him because he was in the right. When the community heard the facts and had a chance to talk the matter over, my assistant maintained, the truth would emerge.

To the Minangkabau, truth is not arbitrary just because it is what people agree is true. Rather, that agreement is proof of va- lidity. In response to my question of why the Minang place such a great emphasis on consensus as the means for arriving at the truth, one informant said, "After discussion who would still maintain that black is white?" Perhaps, too, this view of the nature of truth provides another reason for the absence of factions. If disagreement between segments of the community were generally expected, the idea that truth is established through the process of community agreement would be difficult to maintain. The importance of consensus as an epistemological principle would thus militate against the existence of factions within Bayur.

This perspective about the nature of truth suggests the Islamic belief that the community of Muslims could never unite in error. However, Minang also say that Islamic practices and the most fundamental aspects of adaik (just what these are is hard for them to say) must not be changed even if that change were ordained by consensus. This suggests that the possibility of collective error, however unlikely, is conceivable. However, such a possibility does not seem to trouble them, since they are confident that as Minang they will be mindful of the parameters of Islam and adaik, and therefore in actuality their consensus will not stray from the truth.

Again and again in my discussions about the nature of Minangkabau village life, the paramount and ineluctable importance of the community was stressed. To be a Minangkabau is to be a member of a community. And to be a member in good standing depends on baso basi. Baso basi is both the sign and the means of membership in that community. I talked to various informants about the power of the community to enforce adaik by ostracizing someone who does not regularly subject his behavior to community scrutiny so that it can be appraised and who does not participate socially enough to support community life or who, in his participation, violates adaik and thus is thought to undermine the forms of community life. They also stressed the feeling of helplessness and despair that would inevitably come with such a rejection: "People lie to you, don't respond to your greeting, get up and leave as soon as you sit down. What can you do? What can you say? The only alternative is to leave and go abroad. Perhaps then on a return visit home something of a fresh start can be made."

If someone has committed a major breach of adaik, exclusion from the community may be permanent. I was told of one marriage which violated clan exogamy (a form of marriage, incidentally, which my informants had previously indicated was permissible according to the adaik of certain other Minang communities). Because of the subsequent outrage, the couple went abroad, and, even some years later on their first return to the village, no one except their immediate family would speak to them. There could be no alternative for them, I was told with grim satisfaction, but a permanent sojourn abroad.

To be a member of the community requires continual demonstrations of baso basi, and for those who are deficient in baso basi, as well as in other aspects of adaik, the community withdraws *its* baso basi: failure to observe the social forms is reciprocated. (There may be economic pressure as well. It is difficult for a person rejected by the community to hire help, not so much because workers are so offended that they wish to pass up paid employment, but because they are afraid that others will criticize them if they work for such a person. And what, I was asked rhetorically, is such a disfavored person to do when his roof leaks?) Baso basi does, in fact, primarily concern only a limited portion of adaik—the portion concerned most directly with comportment—but it is stressed so much, I suggest, because it is seen as indicating willingness to conform to adaik in its entirety. Specifically, that one asks others to join in eating, that one offers cigarettes around, that one speaks respectfully to seniors and especially to panghulu, that one maintains respectful reserve with parents-in-law and one's senior matrilineal kin, that one sits or passes others who are sitting in a prescribed way is not only behavior valued for itself, but is taken as an indication of willingness to subscribe to the most general system of constraints—of social form—that comprises adaik.

In the Western or at least the American view, many of these manners, if presented as requirements, would often seem burdensome, distinctly artificial, and furthermore in no fundamental way demonstrative of a person's real worth—his character. But because for the Minangkabau all that can ever be known about someone is his external behavior, the only thing Minang society can hope to do is to demand external conformity. Minangkabau are only those who are willling to act like Minangkabau. The great importance of baso basi resides in its role as the sign and the primary means of that conformity.

Chapter Three
The Composition of the Community

The community has thus far been regarded as largely an undifferentiated unit held together by the experience of living and compelling others to live according to local adaik, an adaik which receives its most mundane expression in the form of baso basi. There are, however, significant differences in the degree to which baso basi and constraint generally are observed, and these differences provide at least a partial basis for the delineation of social categories. The Minang social typology of males includes foreign hippies who display no baso basi and thus are, in Minang eyes, totally unconstrained; youth who show a minimal level of baso basi but are only imperfectly constrained; inmarried men—*urang sumando*—who, because they have acquired the responsibilities of marriage, are extremely constrained, particularly with their inlaws; rowdies—*parewa*—who are men of marriageable age but who have usually not married and who continue to display much of the lack of constraint characteristic of youth; and panghulu, who are the titleholders of the matrilineages and observe the highest and most consistent standards of baso basi.

HIPPIES

As I have mentioned, one of the first questions I was asked when I came to Bayur was what did I think of hippies. And one of the first and most important judgments made about me by the people of Bayur was that I was not a hippy. Any individual from the West who does not conform to Minangkabau standards of dress and deportment is likely to be regarded as a hippy. Most of those pointed out to me as hippies struck me as rather ordinary Western tourists,

dressed in casual comfort for sightseeing in the tropics and displaying an understandable curiosity about their surroundings. However, from the Minang perspective these individuals were profoundly
lacking in baso basi. One elderly Minang man delivered the following diatribe against them, his voice filled with moral loathing.
"Hippies are unconstrained (*bebas*): they are loiterers who do not
follow law or custom; they lack religion as a guide to conduct—
are neither Catholic nor Protestant [much less Muslim]; men and
women wear tight shorts, and women wear tight, revealing blouses;
men and women travel together even though not married, sleep
any place they want, do anything they desire." Others in talking
about hippies referred to their unkempt appearance, comparing
them to animals.

Quite clearly those regarded as hippies did not observe Minangkabau social forms, but even in a relatively popular tourist area
such as Lake Maninjau, not more than a few hippies a month would
walk up the road from the usual bus stop into Bayur. Why, then,
all the fuss about a few foreigners who did not conform to Minang
standards of conduct? The concern was that hippies would have a
corrupting influence on Minangkabau youth.

YOUTH

Minang traditionally expect their youth—that is, unmarried young
men—to be unsettled, and it is in part a response to their perceptions of this stage of life that they expect young men to spend
several years in their late teens abroad. There they gain experience
in the world and are seasoned by having to face the necessity of
supporting themselves. They thereby sufficiently prove themselves
as potential providers so that on their return to the village they
may be sought after as grooms. But while they are still in the village
and are unmarried dependents, they are often the subject of blanket
distrust. It is not that village youth have lacked adequate discipline;
it is rather that they simply *cannot* be adequately disciplined. Most
of them are not thought to be especially reprehensible as individuals
because the behavior of youth is just the way the youth behaves.

I was repeatedly warned not to keep my possessions in my office,
where they would be in sight and reach of the local youth, and on

no account were they to be admitted to my inner chambers. When I asked if this caution should apply to older men as well, I was told that it was primarily the young men who are always grabbing, wanting, taking. Most older men did not constitute such a threat. The image of youth was of only imperfectly constrained desire and energy.

The lodgings the mayor found for me were directly across the street from his office because he felt that he could thus protect me better from the annoyances and depredations of the youth who, he (correctly) assumed, would be drawn to me as a source of Western allure. Late one evening he and the municipal secretary called on me. The mayor was leaving town for several days and was concerned because he thought that without his constraining presence the Bayur youth would try to take advantage of me. His counsel was delivered in the most serious tones, as he sought to convince me of how untrustworthy the youth were. Significantly, he attacked them for their lack of baso basi. Specifically, he cited their loud talk and the way they sat around on my porch with their legs up in the air like "cowboys." And as if all this were not bad enough in itself, it was taking place on the main street, directly across from the mayor's office. It thus constituted an act of disrespect to him, as well as to the other older people in town. He then reminded me that youth tended to steal things and added that they took drugs. Finally he warned me that some of them had magic powers, powers that not only gave them personal invulnerability but could be used to make others sick or mad.

In this attack he thus linked lack of baso basi, theft, drug taking, and sorcery. All of these were manifestations of inadequate social constraint. Finally, and in a sense summarizing these failings, he told me explicitly that youth were not well informed about adaik and for this reason they were not good persons (*budi baiak*).

I got the impression from the older members of the community that they were more concerned about the waywardness of Minang youth in the present than they had been in the past. While listening to their periodic complaints, I sometimes suggested that Minang youth had always constituted a problem in the village. There was agreement with this, but then it was pointed out that currently Minangkabau culture was under great pressure from the West.

Never before had the West been so intrusive, so appealing to the Minang youth, with its attractive goods, fashions, rock music, and the like. The hippies, with their lack of restraint, were seen as particularly threatening because their example weakened the already minimal restraint of Minang youth.

MARRIED MEN

For most but not all young men, the period of youthful irresponsibility ends when they get married and fall under the powerful constraints inherent in becoming a husband, son-in-law, or brother-in-law—an *urang sumando*.

The position of urang sumando is deeply embedded in the Minangkabau version of matrilineality, an arrangement that gives women, especially old women, a remarkable control over property and, in addition, considerable power within a very wide domestic sphere. Women control ancestral property: they own the houses, control the use of and income from inherited land, and make the decision to pawn ancestral property if it becomes necessary. (Tanner 1971 documents fully the extent of women's domestic power.) As a consequence, Minang men, unlike those in the more common matrilineal arrangement, have little authority over their sisters or mothers even though they are partially responsible for their support, especially if the sisters or mothers are divorced or widowed.

After marriage the residence of the couple is usually matrilocal, at least initially. Inside his wife's house a man is treated with considerable deference. He is not allowed to help with household chores and he is treated with great baso basi. During marriage and death rituals, he is often given the rather important role of spokesman for his wife's family. The Minang say that ritual prominence is a measure of the honor given him in his wife's house, but this honor, as well as the deference he receives in daily life, is based on distance: he is an appropriate spokesman for his wife's family because he himself is not a full member of that family and thus can mediate between it and the outside. As a perpetual guest in his wife's house, the urang sumando, despite recent changes to be discussed later, still has little authority over his wife or much voice in daily household affairs.

The most difficult aspect of his role concerns his relationship with his parents-in-law. Minang residence patterns are such that sisters—and female matrikin generally—very often are close neighbors. An urang sumando, therefore, has frequent contact not only with his wife's mother but with his wife's mother's sisters as well. All these women are said to scrutinize the son-in-law very closely; they judge him particularly by the amount of his financial contribution to his household. Nor does there appear to be any solidarity among urang sumando of either the same or adjacent generations within a household. A man treats his father-in-law with the same wary baso basi as he treats his mother-in-law; males married to sisters see each other as rivals for the approval of the parents-in-law and feel that their respective economic contributions are always subject to unfavorable comparison.

Furthermore, there is constraint between a man and his sister's husband, in part rooted in a strong avoidance between brother and sister in sexual matters. As a result, a man usually cannot find refuge even in his own matrilineal house.

Divorce is frequent. (Naim 1973 calculates Minang divorce to be the highest in Indonesia.) Urang sumando are sensitive to slurs from their parents-in-law and frequently leave home for that reason. During my fieldwork, a friend who often stopped in to see me on his way to work came by one day much earlier than usual because he had spent the night sleeping uncomfortably in a coffee shop. He was obviously upset and, although not particularly forthcoming, did say that his parents-in-law had begun to suggest that he was no longer welcome in the house and should move out. This case was of interest in part because the mother-in-law was not actually the mother of my friend's wife. The real mother had died several years before, and her ancestral property—her rice land and house— was inherited, as is customary, by her daughters. The mother's sister, who at the time of my research was considered my friend's mother-in-law, had her house next door and had begun acting as the senior woman of the neighboring household. She was there a great deal of the time and, incidentally, acted as a hostess when I had dinner there at my friend's invitation. (Because of the peripheral position of the urang sumando, very rarely will a man invite someone into his wife's house.) No one saw anything anomalous in her prominent role in what had been her sister's household.

My friend's immediate problem, it seemed to me, originated in his mother-in-law's circumstances. Her husband was in ill health and consequently was unable to fulfill satisfactorily his own responsibility as urang sumando to provide for himself and his wife. The mother-in-law and her husband had been criticizing my friend for not contributing enough money to his wife to enable her in turn to contribute a surplus to them, and my friend was thus under additional pressure. He was already providing food not only for his wife and two children but for his wife's unmarried younger sister and her older married sister. The latter had just returned from abroad in a manic-depressive state (the result of sorcery, it was thought) and was not being adequately supported by her own husband, who had already returned abroad. (Her mother's brother might have helped her if he had not been poor and abroad himself.) My friend felt he was doing his best to be a responsible urang sumando, but he simply could not financially carry the whole family. His response to this most recent escalation of pressure was to absent himself from the household. He stressed to me that he had no quarrel whatsoever with his wife; rather, the difficulty had come to lie with her parents. However, during the week he stayed away from home he did not communicate at all with his wife, avoiding her as well as her parents.

The situation is typical for Minangkabau men. Their best efforts to provide are often not enough, in part because their obligations may expand. But even if they do provide, they never win an entirely secure place in their wife's home.[1] Marriages come apart, or at least experience chronic strain, because of the expectations and often active interference of the wife's parents. An urang sumando usually feels that he is welcome only as long as he is able to make a strong financial contribution. It follows that if the position of a young active urang sumando is precarious, it is even more so for one who is old and infirm. The husband of my companion's grandmother,

1. A parallel situation elsewhere in Sumatra is described in Siegel's 1969 study of Atjeh.

whom I met during my first evening in Bayur, clearly felt such insecurity.

The role of urang sumando is frequently described in conversation by both men and women as a very difficult one. The propensity of affines to find fault with an urang sumando is suggested by the existence of a folk typology that lists the various ways in which an urang sumando may prove to be unsatisfactory. Urang sumando can, for example, resemble a noisy fly which creates a nuisance by buzzing about and getting into things that do not properly concern it. Popular songs also refer to the pressures under which the urang sumando lives.

In some respects, the role may have become even more demanding in recent years with the change in the relative importance of a man's affinal and matrilineal obligations. Circumstances have so changed that a man, if he is pressed by time and money as he is sure to be, will slight his responsibilities as a mother's brother or brother in favor of his responsibilities as father and husband. In part this shift in primary responsibility has come about because it is increasingly common for nuclear families to go abroad. Consequently, for long periods of time a man is likely to be physically separated from his sister and her children, who are thus effectively removed from his influence. Correspondingly, the father has become more central in family life—whether abroad or in the village—than is reported to have been the case in the past, to the extent that he is now supposed to be entirely responsible for the support of his wife and children, including, for instance, his children's school fees. Moreover, he is now supposed to pay for the support of his children in the case of divorce.

Such changes in the distribution of male responsibilities may well have progressed further in Bayur at the time of my study than in many other Minangkabau communities. For instance, there is currently little mention in Bayur of chronic financial pressure placed on a man by his sisters, evidently still a source of marital tension elsewhere. I suspect that the extent of these changes is partly a result of the fact that Bayur has long been dependent on the outside world and has, in addition, long been subject to the patriarchal influences of Reformist Islam.

That such changes in patterns of male responsibility have been under way in Bayur for some time is also suggested by changes in residence pattern early in this century. Prior to a great fire in 1911, most of the people in Bayur lived in large houses that were identified with particular matrilineages. These houses contained a huge common room running the length and about half the width of the house, with most of the remaining half taken up separate one-room apartments for each couple, composed of a woman of the matrilineage and her inmarried husband. These houses were not rebuilt after the fire, according to my informants, for two related reasons. The first was that the mother's brother no longer had the power to command sufficient labor from his sister's sons to complete such a large project. The second reason was that few men, in fact, still wished to live in these big houses. The destruction by fire of most of the big houses provided men with a welcome opportunity to build smaller houses where they could set up more private and autonomous households. In these separate dwellings, a father and husband would have somewhat more to say about family life than before.

However, even in these smaller houses the contemporary husband or father still remains vulnerable, for he is still regarded as an urang sumando. The house itself still is on the wife's land and belongs to her and her daughters in the event of divorce or the husband's death. This is the case whether the house has been built by the husband himself, whether it has been inherited by his wife, or whether, as is sometimes the case, it was built for her by her father. Moreover, the contemporary household often still includes a very observant mother-in-law and perhaps her husband as well.

Because the responsibilities of husbands have actually increased, few men now choose to contract the polygynous marriages permitted by Islam. Most men feel that to acquire an additional wife would simply multiply their difficulties, since there would be an additional household to support and additional parents-in-law to please. Moreover, the jealousy cowives often feel simply would add strain to an already difficult domestic situation.

Although a man eats and sleeps in his wife's house, it is easy to see why he prefers to spend his leisure time elsewhere, in the streets or the coffee shops. The evening custom of men congregating in the public area—of the male part of the community convening daily—is seen by the Minang as partially a product of the urang sumando's circumstances. Minangkabau men, in most cases, simply have no home of their own in which they can fully relax.

Marriage, then, is a decisive step. A Minang man as an urang sumando is very different indeed from an irresponsible youth: he has many obligations; he must observe respectful behavior expressed in baso basi. This baso basi is of a very formal sort which exceeds in constraint that required on all but the most formal of ritual occasions. However, a few men, the parewa, do manage to maintain some of the freedom of their youth either by not marrying at all or by simply evading marital responsibilities. They, too, fulfill a traditional role. Parewa are men who have carried the pattern of rowdy irresponsible youth into their twenties or longer, past the time when most of their peers have married and settled down. They are regarded by other men of the community with ambivalence: distrust, because they still have the lack of constraint of youth, and envy, because they have managed to avoid the constraint of marriage. To become a parewa is, I think, a somewhat disreputable, although not unappealing, alternative to becoming a constrained, watchful, and often anxious urang sumando.

During the time of my study, Bayur had several young men who were clearly parewa, plus a number of older men, some of them married, who were sometimes described as having the spirit of parewa.

PAREWA

Bayur and, I was told, every Minangkabau town has its little gang of parewa. Most of these do not have regular jobs; they continue to eat at home with their parents; and, in Bayur at least, they make their spending money by extorting small sums from drivers of the passing buses. These collections are routine and the sums are small. The bus drivers prefer to pay them rather than risk the retribution of slashed tires, nails scattered across the road, and such; nor would it be feasible to try to mobilize the police. I questioned my informants very closely about whether these parewa extort money from the locals, bother visitors who come to Bayur for the weekly market, or steal from local stores. I was told that they do not. Apparently, the parewa depredations are limited to the passing buses.

My older informants acknowledged that shaking down buses is not admirable behavior. Then, without excusing the parewa for extorting money from bus drivers, they stressed that in case of local crisis such as fire or death these same parewa are the first to come forward and help. Moreover, they defend the village interests and honor against men from neighboring villages. In the recent past, for instance, there had been fights between parewa and other men of neighboring towns about fishing rights in the lake. Until recently Bayur parewa harassed young men from other villages who came courting in Bayur, regarding them as having dishonorable intentions. But eventually, because of the great shortage of marriageable men resulting from the economic pressures which led men in ever greater numbers and for longer duration to work abroad, such suitors were accepted. However, Bayur parewa still make sure that these suitors do not attempt to tarnish the reputation of the local girls.

The people of Bayur tolerate and in some cases applaud the rough behavior of their parewa. One story of local parewa in action, told with some approval, was of a motorcyclist who struck a child in Bayur and then fled from the scene. He was chased by the Bayur parewa and other youth, who were in turn joined by other parewa and youth from the towns along the lake through which the fugitive passed in his flight. Eventually he was captured in the lake itself, given a thorough beating, and only then turned over to the police. When I said that it was standard advice in Bayur to leave the scene of any accident to seek sanctuary with the police, I was told that this particular motorcyclist had apparently not intended to seek such sanctuary. Instead he had tried to conceal his license plate during his escape, an act which further inflamed the people of Bayur, since it suggested that he had no intention of turning himself in.

Amir, a young man in his mid-twenties at the time of my research, was the leading parewa in Bayur. Reputedly the best fighter in town, he would take on all comers. He was also considered rather too stupid to prosper abroad and, in fact, had never gone. His readiness to fight itself was taken, at least by some older men, as a sign of stupidity: it showed that he did not reckon the possibility of incurring serious injuries; it showed that he did not weigh the consequences of his action. As they put it, "His thought is short."

Amir and his several parewa chums, although openly defying their panghulu and mother's brothers when these advised them to find a more reputable and serious livelihood, did observe the minimal standards of baso basi. They were reasonably respectful of their elders (when these were not trying to give them advice); they exchanged appropriate greetings with those they met in the daily late-afternoon perambulations; they observed the basic etiquette associated with eating, drinking, and smoking (even though they did mooch cigarettes far more often than they offered them).

Amir's position as the town's leading parewa had not been unchallenged by others interested in taking over his reputation and gaining control of the local bus "franchise." In fact, his little gang was composed of several former challengers who had come to terms with him and each other. During my fieldwork he encountered a rather serious challenge from two young men, Lan and Mel, just returned to Bayur from several years together abroad.

Whereas Amir and his parewa friends, as toughs, received in accentuated form the same sort of distrust applied to youth, their irresponsibility and impulsiveness were partially offset by their adequate commitment to baso basi. Lan and Mel were very different and immediately overtaxed the tolerance that the people of Bayur usually feel toward their resident parewa. These two were sullen, did not offer or respond to greetings of kin or other residents, stole vegetables from the fields and fish from the ponds for food. Their kin, particularly, were angry with them but could not induce them to behave in a minimally acceptable manner.

Then Lan and Mel began muscling in on the bus franchise, stopping buses on their own for money. They thus constituted a clear challenge to Amir's preeminence. One morning when I got up, the town was buzzing with excitement. During the night Lan and Mel as a team and Amir had been pursuing each other around town and had met up early in the morning. Amir had sustained a stab wound in the back (stabbing in the back was considered distinctly unsportsmanlike); Lan and Mel had fled. Amir had then gone to the clinic in the adjacent town, and soon after he had informed the regional police detachment there of the assault. The police came immediately to Bayur; the local militia were convened, and then police and militia began the search for the two miscreants.

Ordinarily the people of Bayur greatly prefer to settle their own disputes without involving the police, who not only are stationed in a neighboring town toward whom Bayur feels some rivalry, but are largely composed of men from other parts of Indonesia, principally Java. But in this case, because local sentiment had been sufficiently aroused against Lan and Mel for behaving in a uniformly antisocial manner and for showing themselves impervious to the community's disapproval, the people of Bayur were willing to suffer the shame of turning the matter over to the outside authorities.

Lan was apprehended the next day but Mel escaped. After serving a month in the police detachment jail, Lan returned to Bayur, shorn of his long hair, rather subdued, certainly more civil, and for the moment at least apparently not looking for trouble with Amir or anyone else.

I came to know one parewa, Nambo Samsir, as a very old man. Soon after I arrived in Bayur he joined me on my front porch, introduced himself as "Nambo" (grandfather, which everyone did in fact call him), and immediately asked whether I was getting enough to eat. Despite my assurances, he patted my stomach for corroboration. He was very old, but still an extremely sturdy-looking man. Between him and the people of Bayur there was jovial bantering, in which he obviously had the last word. He was, I was told, a bit crude but good-hearted. It also became clear that people were careful not to cross him. In these respects he was typical of parewa.

In his youth he had been one of the few men who never went abroad; instead he became Bayur's leading parewa. It may be significant that my informants in separate conversations about Amir and Nambo Samsir thought to mention that neither had worked abroad. The experience of working abroad is thought to temper youthful energy, presumably so that most young men will become urang sumando rather than parewa. (That Lan and Mel had returned from abroad as parewa would simply confirm the Minangkabau view that youth is difficult to discipline.) In any case, everyone had been afraid of Nambo because of his skill in fighting with fists and knife—and, in fact, even at what he claimed was his age of ninety-five, he still carried a sheath knife. But it was not just his physical skill that made him feared. It was his knowledge of magic. With his magic he could uproot trees, rub his body with red hot chains without being burned, stab himself without injury, and afflict his enemies so that they could not excrete. He also had magic that could so bewitch a husband that he would not know that Nambo had entered his marital bed, a capacity which, given the very strong Minangkabau emphasis on female purity, must touch on deep male fears.

As a youth, then, Nambo was formidable indeed in getting his own way, and he had aroused both disapproval and envy. In his later years he had slowed down some. He was no longer interested in other men's wives and had not remarried when two of his former total of four wives (the maximum allowed by Islamic law) had died. His practice of magic had become largely benign: he made spells to keep rain away from ceremonies, made house sites safe from spirits, and guarded against magical attacks from others. But he was still formidable. He still knew his magic and, moreover, was not likely to be inhibited by religious scruples.

He considered his spiritual redemption a lost cause, for he subscribed to the belief widely held in Bayur that those who have led wicked lives, especially those who have been magicians, have no chance of going to heaven; instead they will be initially reborn as pigs or tigers and, after their death in that form, will go to hell. Nambo was quoted to me as having said that he certainly hoped he would be reborn not as a pig but as a tiger, for as a tiger he would be able to threaten the living. This was a prospect that made people even more reluctant to incur his displeasure. One informant, for instance, was quite explicit to me about this: it was only his fear of Nambo, either alive or dead, that had led him to take him, at Nambo's request, on a long trip—a trip made much more difficult and uncomfortable by Nambo's substantial presence on my informant's small motorcycle.

Yet this account would be incomplete without indicating that the people of Bayur were proud of Nambo: he was a local institution. At least after he had settled down a good deal his past exploits of strength and audacity were seen as demonstrating a forceful individuality. He was regarded as a type of person every town has—a cock of the walk. He exemplified the energetic, assertive male who acts without fear of the consequences, either physical or social. Although a potential or actual source of disorder, he at least observed the social forms—the baso basi—of daily life, and for that reason, as well, perhaps, because everyone was afraid of him, he was able to remain within the community.

Datuak Batuah, too, carried into his adult life something of the parewa spirit, and he became probably the most admired and influential person in Bayur. His attributes were more diverse than Nambo's, but he shared Nambo's reputation for knowledge of magic coupled with physical courage, decisiveness, and audacity.

Datuak Batuah had spent his last working years as the chief of police of a neighboring province. During those years he had been very generous to the people of Bayur who had visited him. On his periodic visits to Bayur he had held open house, offering hospitality to the men and women who thronged to see him.[2]

Shortly after Datuak Batuah was pensioned from the police and returned home to live in Bayur, his panghulu retired from office and he became the new panghulu. ("Datuak" indicates the office of panghulu; "Batuah" is the title which the panghulu of this particular matrilineage always carries.) He quickly became very popular, and was considered to have good judgment and to be conscientious in fulfilling his duties. Datuak Batuah became prominent in community affairs, in contexts ranging from the parent-teachers association to the formal meetings of panghulu. (He also was particularly instrumental in helping me fit into the community.

2. Minang greatly admire anyone who is not only prosperous but shares his prosperity with the community. One such benefactor donated a generator to the mosque, sponsored free performances in Bayur by well-known Minang musicians and, on his most recent visit at least, gave out quantities of 500 rupiah banknotes to street-corner youth. This is spectacular generosity, since even though 500 rupiahs is equivalent to only about $1.25, it is more than a day's pay for many. Such a man is well regarded not only because of his largesse per se but, I think, because his prosperity shows that he has disciplined his potentially anarchic energy, and his generosity shows that he has tempered his self-interest. His actions, then, are valued for the same reasons that baso basi is valued: both are statements of commitment to the community.

For instance, after I had been in Bayur only a few days, he invited me to his house to give me a crash course in the basic requirements of Minang baso basi, particularly concerning the daily etiquette associated with eating, smoking, and greeting.) Because of his experience and skill in public speaking and his control of the highly valued Minangkabau forms of oblique ceremonial speech, he was often called upon to act as master of ceremonies.

Datuak Batuah had still other capabilities. His ridged fingernails indicated considerable physical and magical power: he had reputedly killed a gangster with one blow; he was a curer *(dukun)* of note; he held periodic interviews with tigers in his living room; he held seances and could cause people to become possessed and speak in other voices. He was formidable not only for his knowledge of magic, but for his capacity for strong, quick action.

I was told with considerable relish and admiration of a visit he made to Bayur some years before, while he was still a member of the police. Two brothers had been quarreling about the division of their inheritance, in particular about the disposition of a kerosene pressure lamp. Datuak Batuah came upon these quarreling brothers and asked whether either of them was willing to give the other half the lamp's value in cash. Neither was, so Datuak Batuah placed the lamp in the middle of the road, drew his gun, and shot the lamp to pieces. That settled the dispute.

Datuak Batuah's command of magic, his physical courage, and his decisiveness were presented to me as parewa characteristics. I was also told that he still enjoyed the traditional parewa (and anti-Islamic) pursuits of gambling and cockfighting. Clearly his high standing in the community rested in part on his continuing to possess the spirit of a parewa.

Minangkabau male culture values audacity in the form of physical courage, toughness, and the ability to defend one's interests verbally and, if necessary, physically. Charles Bronson and, before him, Marlon Brando, was at the time of my research a cultural figure, depicted while engaged in various ruggedly masculine activities on calendars and in advertising. Cars and motorcycles often carried large decals of crossed rifles. Young men going abroad for the first time were advised by their fathers not to look for fights but certainly not to run from them either. Men discussed with pride their guerrilla exploits during the 1958 insurrection, when West Sumatra attempted to break away from the central Indonesian government.

Amir, Lan and Mel, Nambo Samsir, and Datuak Batuah all derived prestige from their parewa capacity for strong, dramatic, and potentially violent action, but it is well to differentiate among them. It is unlikely that Amir, Lan and Mel, or others of the current crop of full-time parewa, will derive other than the most passing importance from their quickness to fight. Such impulsiveness is always regarded with at least some suspicion and is tolerated only as long as there is minimal conformity to standards of baso basi. Amir and Lan and Mel represent a short continuum from the barely acceptable to the totally unacceptable. Once the period of youthful strength is past, this untempered audacity is considered not only somewhat inappropriate and unbecoming (although not entirely unappealing) but rather foolish. In fact, most parewa do settle down as befits men of their age: Amir's immediate predecessors all have married and accepted domestic constraints. It is only someone like Nambo Samsir, with his exceptionally robust physique and his reputation for magic, who can continue to carry the hair-trigger formidability of a parewa into middle age. The most that an older man should ordinarily show of his parewa past, or his response to that aspect of the Minangkabau tradition which values audacity, is that he have the spirit of a parewa.

This spirit can be shown in various ways. Some older men, for instance, habitually carry knives; some may customarily carry a sarong folded into a narrow strip across their shoulder to be used in protection against knife attack. (The folded sarong may also simply mean that the man is on his way to prayers.) The parewa spirit is shown less obviously, although more commonly, simply by cultivating a reputation as someone who, although not looking for trouble, should not be trifled with.

PANGHULU

A panghulu, regarded by the Minangkabau as a major source of order, is in contrast to the parewa, who is too quick to fight and often a source of disorder. A panghulu is always a male; he settles problems ranging from fist fights between young men, to serious marital squabbles, to land disputes among the hundred or so members of the matrilineage who are his constituency. But although what he does is often very useful, most villagers could stay out of trouble or settle their grievances without relying on the intercession of a panghulu. For instance, they could—and do—have recourse to their mothers' brothers, the police or the courts. Or, as yet another alternative, they could call on the mayor to intervene in a dispute, especially because he might be called in anyway if the panghulu could not bring about a settlement.

Two additional circumstances might minimize the contemporary usefulness of the panghulu. During the Dutch administration, as I have mentioned, the panghulu were known to abuse their role as defenders of adaik, usually in permitting sale of ancestral land for their own benefit. Currently the panghulu, because of the pressures of making their own living, are somewhat less attentive to their duties than they traditionally were. However, despite agreement with me that the role had once been severely abused and was now reduced, that other agents were available for the settlement of disputes, and that individuals did not need panghulu to manage their own affairs, at least while abroad, everyone asserted with great conviction that the panghulu were still absolutely essential to Minang life.

The panghulu remain the major source of order in Minangkabau society, despite the presence of alternative sources of order, because they represent—in fact are the incarnation of—constraint: not, of course, constraint per se, but constraint in the Minangkabau mode. Panghulu are exemplars of baso basi in particular and adaik in general. They are selected by members of their matrilineages to become panghulu in part because of their knowledge of adaik. (A discussion of the process of selection and the nature of the matrilineal groups involved will be given in chapter 6.) With this knowledge, they can remind disputants or malefactors of their adaik obligations. Moreover, as panghulu they often use very allusive, flowery speech, laced with traditional aphorisms and metaphors. This combination of formality and condensed wisdom cools passions as well as counsels, so that an individual is usually thereby brought properly back under the umbrella of adaik.

Panghulu, then, are effective in bringing order, in part because they exemplify order. This does not mean, of course, that some panghulu are not more effective, more popular, or more respected than others. Very occasionally dissatisfaction is so great that someone changes his panghulu—a change which necessitates the complex procedure of changing one's matrilineage. In each of the only two cases of this sort that I was able to find—one concerned a man, the other, a woman—the dissatisfaction stemmed from the way the panghulu settled an inheritance dispute.[3] Moreover, panghulu are not always able to rely on the power of their refined comportment to bring order but sometimes must talk very directly and forcefully with recalcitrants. Not all panghulu are willing or able to do this, and not always is such action effective. I have heard men boast that their panghulu were afraid of them and hence would not interfere with their lives; and, indeed, in modern times panghulu have few sanctions to bring if their strongly worded advice is ignored. About all they can do in this case is what the two panghulu of Lan and Mel did: they simply failed to intervene and let the police, with their heavier hand, take immediate charge.

Even though panghulu may have become less effective than they once were—and it is hard to tell precisely what their effectiveness was before the Dutch increased it in some respects and reduced it in others—panghulu have remained relatively fixed points in Minang experience. They continue to demonstrate the nature of baso basi and, more generally, of adaik. Hence they provide a condensed image of what it is to be a Minangkabau. They also contribute to a more specific sense of personal identity by providing part of an individual's social location within a community. Everyone in Bayur has a panghulu, even those who marry into Bayur or those who visit for an extended period of time. Everyone is the "child" of a particular panghulu, an *anak buah*, and is often referred to in that way. Thus, to be the anak buah of Datuak Batuah, for

3. In changing their matrilineal affiliation, this man and woman relinquished all rights to inherit matrilineal property, including land. However, as a result of the decisions of their panghulu, they felt they were already largely disinherited. Since everyone in Bayur must have a matrilineal affiliation, each had to petition another panghulu to be granted a new—if nominal—matrilineal membership.

example, is to be more than his responsibility. It is to have him to turn to if there is a problem; it is to have him as an image of proper conduct; it is to have a social location in Bayur.

Minang society includes at one extreme, although with misgivings, the energy and relative freedom from constraint of youth and parewa—but not of hippies—and at the other extreme, the sometimes painful and almost stifling formality of panghulu. A few individuals such as Datuak Batuah might achieve a Minang male ideal by coupling the audacity of the parewa with the extreme baso basi of the panghulu. For those encompassed within Minang society it is baso basi, whether minimally or maximally expressed, that is the sign as well as the means of their inclusion in a single community.

For the Minang, baso basi can facilitate, please, impede, and annoy, just as etiquette does in the West. However, for the Minang, baso basi is so absolutely fundamental to their view and experience of social life because it is regarded as a manifestation of adaik, which is—as we shall see even more clearly in the next chapter— the proper and the true. Baso basi is observed not simply to avoid censure but because it is right.

PART III
ADAIK AND EPISTEMOLOGY

Chapter 4
The Nature of Interpretation

Adaik defines the nature of Minangkabau community life by providing a conceptual foundation for all discussion about behavior. Informants did differ considerably in their knowledge of the details of adaik and in their capacity to explain what aspects of adaik meant. Nonetheless, discussions with both experts and nonexperts about what a particular custom meant, about why central ceremonial details were as they were, and about why one sort of activity was acceptable to or required by the community, frequently included the statement that, moreover, such was adaik. Likewise, discussion about why a particular practice was not followed or why an individual's action was not acceptable to the community often ended with a statement that it simply was not permissible, was not in accord with adaik.

A person of good repute was defined to me as someone who knows adaik, although he might not necessarily be an authority on adaik. One of the most effective ways that children can be controlled when misbehaving, even by foreigners, is to shame them by saying that they do not know adaik. To assert that an adult does not know adaik is a most serious insult. Virtually all aspects of public conduct concern adaik and are thus of importance to the community.

Just as panghulu are expected to know and observe more elaborate baso basi than any other group within the community, so also they are expected to know more about adaik and be more punctilious in their adherence to adaik than any other group. Panghulu are thus expected to exhibit to the greatest extent the traditional forms of constraint in their daily and ritual deportment, as well as to demonstrate to the greatest extent through word and deed the traditional principles and activities which comprise Minangkabau custom in general.

Shortly after my arrival in Bayur, I attended a session of the local panghulu who had met to discuss and thus enhance their understanding of adaik. At the time, I was told that these meetings were weekly occurrences, but in fact this was the only meeting of this sort which took place during my study. (Panghulu also meet collectively to adjudicate those disputes, usually concerning property settlements, which have not been satisfactorily resolved by the panghulu of the individual disputants. No such meeting took place during my study.)

The mayor, himself a panghulu, moderated the meeting on adaik. He began the meeting by writing a number of lists and aphorisms on the blackboard at the head of the room. One list was of the "three cords" (adaik, religion, and government) which bind together Minang society; one aphorism concerned the composition of a well-run village with youth, men, women, and panghulu all fulfilling their proper roles; another concerned the relationship between matrilineal seniors and juniors. All of these must have been very familiar to those present at the meeting, since I often heard them expressed when people were later explaining adaik to me. My command of Minangkabau at that time was not sufficient for me to follow the discussion on these points at the meeting, but I was very struck by the measured and controlled courtesy—the baso basi— with which everyone made his remarks and by the smiles of quiet contentment and the frequent nods of assent with which these remarks on largely familiar subjects were greeted. The meeting could not be compared to a seminar in which new perspectives were being introduced and conflicting views were worked out. It was like a religious service in which a congregation was accepting, indeed welcoming, truths.

In an effort to expand their knowledge of the truths of adaik, the Bayur panghulu invited Idroes Hakimi, whose title was Datuak Rajo Panghulu, to come and lecture. Datuak Rajo Panghulu was one of several major Minang experts on adaik and was the currently elected president of the association of West Sumatran panghulu. His visit was heralded, and a few out-of-town guests, a reasonable number of local men and women, and I attended. After introductions, reports, and brief speeches by and to the local military and civil authorities also in attendance, Datuak Rajo Panghulu began by remarking that he had clarified adaik over the radio, in various articles, and in person in over six hundred places in West Sumatra; but this was his first appearance in Bayur. Since time was short, he would just present essential information about adaik.

The range of topics he covered was vast, and in going over the transcript of the tape I made, I was unable to find any pattern of organization. He gave traditional aphorisms about the relationship of Islam to adaik, about marriage practices, about the difficulties a panghulu faces in providing leadership for his matrilineal juniors, about the fruitful nature of discussion among panghulu, and about the necessity of keeping teenaged boys and girls separate from each other. Interspersed with these aphorisms were observations on the centrality of women in the Minangkabau matrilineal system, on the practice of avoidance between brothers-in-law, on the kind of encouragement panghulu should give their matrilineal juniors so that they may become financially independent, on the importance of impartiality in the settlement of disputes—and much, much more.

Datuak Rajo Panghulu was a learned man: his lecture included long quotations in Arabic from the Koran (he was also a religious scholar); he dropped in phrases in English (e.g., "dedication of life"); he mentioned world historical figures (e.g., Hitler and Napoleon, both of whom met their demise because of excessive indulgence with women, an indulgence for which women seemed to be held responsible).

But the aspect of his erudition that was of particular interest to his audience was the unfamiliar detail he inserted about adaik. For instance, virtually every Minang knows the names of the two panghulu who are thought to have originated the contrasting democratic and aristocratic systems of Minang local government. Datuak Rajo Panghulu, however, gave names of two panghulu who had preceded these two. He also included the original meaning of *Datuak*, the original pronunciation of *adaik*, the size and location of the first Minangkabau settlement, and the circumstances of the first human burial. All of this information, my informants later assured me, was important. Especially, these facts were important for panghulu to know.

Excluding the break for lunch and noon prayer, he spoke nonstop for four hours to an undiminished audience. Both the men and the women present (many fewer women than men) were extremely attentive, even though most of what he said was well known to them (e.g., that the Minangkabau have a matrilineal system in which inheritance favors women). Although there was no problem hearing, the audience leaned forward in their chairs, a glow of contentment on their faces. Some took notes; occasionally someone would ask Datuak Rajo Panghulu to repeat something that had been missed. Certain evocative words such as *adaik* and *mupakaik* (consensus) were repeated again and again. Datuak Rajo Panghulu was like a preacher pouring truth into his congregation. I did not sense the presence of critical minds, weighing and evaluating what he was saying. Everyone, not just the panghulu, seemed fully content at being Minangkabau. This was the same atmosphere that had been present, although perhaps not in such undiluted form, at the meeting of the local panghulu several months before.

Although the meetings of the Bayur panghulu to discuss adaik and the visit of someone of Datuak Rajo Panghulu's stature were formal and somewhat exceptional events, much the same kind of presentation and interpretation of adaik that took place on these occasions also took place casually and sporadically in daily life.

Minangkabau men, particularly those who were middle-aged and older, took pride in their ability to give me explanations of what various aspects of adaik meant and often volunteered these meanings to me and to each other. Indeed, very often older men would approach me and, after introducing themselves, promptly launch into an exposition of Minang adaik, including a specification of what were the distinctive aspects of Bayur adaik in particular. The women and younger men, and sometimes children, although less likely than older men to volunteer information about adaik, when asked in the absence of someone such as a senior male thought to be more knowledgeable, were often able to produce some sort of interpretation. If unable to do so, they would usually refer me to someone known to be expert on adaik, or just say that the older men knew the answer I was seeking.

Datuak Rajo Panghulu was according to local opinion far more expert than anyone in Bayur; and within Bayur three or four men were considered to be significantly more expert than the rest. An understanding of the basis of their reputations leads to an examination of basic Minangkabau premises about reality: the nature of truth, the nature of the community and the nature of an individual's relationship to the community. The way that adaik is interpreted and how those interpretations are evaluated says a great deal about the significance of adaik itself.

The following examples are typical of the style, as well as the substance, of Minang interpretation of adaik. That these interpretations often seem profoundly unconvincing to the Western investigator suggests that interpretation—that is, explanation—follows rather different premises for the Minang than for the Westerner.

THE CASE OF THE FOUR TOWERS

One evening I was chatting on my front porch with my young (twenty-seven-year-old) assistant Jhon and two men in late middle age, both of whom, like most of their peers, considered themselves sufficiently well versed in adaik to act as my mentors. One of the older men remarked that the four towers of the Bayur mosque standing directly opposite us had originally referred to the four traditional categories in a Minang community: the panghulu, the *cadiak pandai* (intellectuals), the *Imam Chatib* (religious leaders), and the *parik paga* (an indigenous police). The central tower stood for the unity of these four categories, which together formed the community. But, he continued, in the present day the parik paga no longer existed: their law-keeping role had been taken over by the Indonesia national police and the local militia. Consequently, the tower which had originally stood for the parik paga now stood for the Bundo Kandueng, a newly formed women's organization. Moreover, as a parallel to the adaik meaning, the four towers also represented four schools of Islamic practice, only one of which was followed in Bayur. However, each of these four schools had, I was assured, the same basic objectives, as demonstrated by the one central tower.

THE CASE OF THE FIVE-SIDED PACKET

In preparation for the elaborate ritual observed in the ascension of a man to the panghulu title of his matrilineage, small, intricately folded, five-sided paper packets are constructed and filled with betel nut ingredients. These packets, called *kaban*, are then delivered to the other panghulu in Bayur as part of their invitation to attend the ritual. Several Minangkabau men, one of them a panghulu, volunteered the meaning of these packets. The first said that the five sides stood for the five ingredients contained in the mixture. The man actually constructing the packets at the time said that they stood for Pancasila, the five principles first formulated during Sukarno's administration as the foundation of the Republic of Indonesia. I then began to ask others about this: one man also said Pancasila; another said that this five-sided packet, when looked at from any single angle, showed only three sides and that these three sides stood for the three raja of Minangkabau's past. Eventually I asked a local schoolteacher, Sutan Zara Endah, considered by many to be Bayur's leading adaik expert. I began by telling him the various interpretations of the five sides I had already heard.

Sutan Zara Endah was temporarily puzzled and said that he would have to make inquiries. But, he assured me, the five sides of the packet meant something. Several days later I heard him telling a group of men that the five sides stood for four different types of speech plus religion. (He may well have broached this topic because he saw me approaching the group.) There are actually at least two sets of four types of speech; one set refers to the way one talks to members of different social categories; another set refers to the way one talks about adaik. It was not apparent to my assistant when I told him of this conversation which of the four types of speech was being referred to here.

THE CASE OF THE UNHUSKED RICE

For a collective house-raising a general invitation goes out through the village to both men and women. The men contribute labor; the women bring unhusked rice, which is piled on a mat near the house site. Since the usual gift on ceremonial occasions is husked rice,

I inquired why unhusked rice was appropriate for a house-raising. The first man I asked said that unhusked rice was brought because it could be used as seed and would thus increase and better help cover the expense of a house-raising. Another man said it was a more useful gift because rice keeps much longer in unhusked form. I then asked my assistant, who said he did not know. I suggested to him that unhusked rice and the way it is stored may be associated in Minang thought with the house itself, since large exterior granaries were often mentioned to me as a feature of traditional architecture and the smaller storage bins were often pointed out to me as I was shown around inside a traditional house. My assistant found my explanation plausible. Clearly there was no standard explanation and each of us was simply thinking about the differences between these two forms of rice and then attempting to find some link between these and the occasion of a house-raising.

THE CASE OF THE BRASS URN

Minangkabau explanations often involve presentations of folk etymologies. I inquired, for instance, about the meaning of a brass urn called *carano*, often filled with the ingredients necessary in preparing a plug of betel nut, and a lavishly decorated cloth into which circles of glass are set, called *lalamak*. The two usually appear together with the lalamak covering the carano as a sign of respectful hospitality at ceremonies. Guests are encouraged to help themselves to the enclosed ingredients.

When I asked what the carano meant I was given its etymology: its meaning lies in its original form which is *caran*, "to quarrel," and *inyo*, "he/she." Carano thus, I was told, had the original meaning of he/she quarrels. If two individuals are quarreling, then the carano will be brought forth and the quarrel will cease. The term *lalamak* had the original form of *alam alam mamak*. *Alam* is "realm," *mamak* is "mother's brother/male matrilineal senior." When *alam alam mamak* was pronounced rapidly, the words ran together, producing the word *lalamak*. The association of *lalamak* and *carano* is that if there is quarreling, the mamak comes and puts an end to it. Why the betel nut mixture? I asked. Because if two disputants eat betel nut together they will be reconciled, the quarrel ended.

THE CASE OF THE CLAN NAME

This case further illustrates the Minang penchant for explanation by etymology. Minang agree that there are two very general political traditions in Minang culture, each of which stemmed from a primal panghulu. These two panghulu were half-brothers, sharing a Minang mother: one, Datuak Ketemanggungan, had a Javanese king as father and founded the aristocratic Koto-Piliang tradition; the other, Datuak Perpatih nan Sabatang, had a Minangkabau commoner as father (who, incidentally, traveled widely abroad) and founded the democratic Bodi-Caniago tradition. (Koto and Piliang, Bodi and Caniago are all names of matriclans—*suku*—which appear in Minang villages of both traditions. Bayur, for instance, has members of Koto, Piliang, and Caniago, as well as three other suku, and follows the democratic tradition. These two traditions differ primarily in selection procedure for panghulu and in seating arrangements at meetings. Each was also associated with a somewhat distinctive legal code, but after West Sumatra became subject to the laws of the Republic of Indonesia these legal differences no longer held. My informants thought that the differences between these two traditions were no longer of much importance because all places in the republic followed a pattern of democracy.)

Among the information about adaik volunteered to me early in my stay was the meaning—the origin—of the terms *Koto-Piliang* and *Bodi-Caniago*. Although everyone agreed that one referred to an aristocratic and one to a democratic tradition, there was little agreement on the origin of the terms themselves.

Datuak Batuah, who obviously aspired to be regarded as an expert in adaik and was, in fact, considered well informed, said that Koto-Piliang was really a contraction of *kato kato nan di piliah*, which means literally "the talk that is chosen." This, he said, referred to the democratic process of discussion and consensus. Bodi-Caniago was derived from *budi nan di curigo*, which means "intentions which are suspect." The aristocratic Bodi-Caniago government, he continued, was not good because it created suspicion and mistrust and was therefore replaced by the democratic Koto-Piliang form. The difficulty in this argument which seemed to have escaped Datuak Batuah at the time, was that he had turned these traditions around and given an etymology in such a way that Koto-Piliang was democratic and Bodi-Caniago aristocratic. This goes directly counter to what everyone else said was the case.

I asked another older man who also considered himself well versed in adaik about the meaning of Koto-Piliang and Bodi-Caniago. It all began, he said, when the two early panghulu were arguing and the one with the aristocratic father said "I chose," *hambo piliah*, and the name Piliang thus came from *piliah*, "to choose." He could choose because he was descended from the raja. Caniago was from *niaga*, meaning "traders:" these were the commoners who had come into Minangkabau territory to trade. I then asked where the terms *Koto* and *Bodi* had come from. The reply was that these were just names that were applied when the Piliang and Caniago groups got too large to be governed easily and were thus subdivided.

Sutan Zara Endah, when I asked him about these two terms, told me, as had the rest, of the two half-brothers but explicitly rejected the derivation that Koto-Piliang came from *piliah*. He said that the original term was *parahiang*, which was Sanscrit for "many gods." By the time this term had traveled through Indochina, the *r* had been dropped—people in those areas could not pronounce it—and the term became *palahiang* and then *Piliang*. He said that if you know Sanscrit, have read the histories and various books, then it is clear that *kato kato nan di piliah* is not the correct derivation. What about Bodi-Caniago, I asked. That was from *budi nan di curigo*—meaning "intentions which are suspect." This, Sutan Zarah Enda said, was the conclusion reached by Datuak Ketemanggungan, who thought that Datuak Perpatih nan Sabatang held suspicious thought about him, as the two were not getting along well together.

The first of these explanations attempts to deal with all four terms in a roughly comparable way, but the fact that it contradicts certain well-established views associating one pair of terms with an aristocratic and the other pair with a democratic tradition is overlooked. The second explanation accounts for the link between the terms and the political tradition but largely ignores the meaning of *Bodi* and *Koto;* the last explanation provides very dissimilar origins for each pair of terms and also shows rather clearly the value that Sutan Zara Endah places on providing by means of his scholarship an interpretation that is distinctive. These explanations appear fragmented and often internally inconsistent. Furthermore, Minang are unconcerned if an explanation does not fit with other interpretations of their culture.

THE CASE OF THE FIGURES OF SPEECH

Figures of speech—*kiasan*—are traditional sources of wisdom, used to convey and interpret adaik on both formal and informal occasions. Formal speech may, in fact, consist of little more than streams of these traditional images. They are valued because they allow the speaker to be oblique and are thus indicative of refinement, of constraint. Men pride themselves on their knowledge of figures of speech just as they pride themselves on their knowledge of other aspects of adaik.

Most figures of speech contain images of nature, images which seem often to be taken in a largely literal way. In his address, Datuak Rajo Panghulu several times repeated a phrase which I was to hear often in Bayur, *Alam takambang jadi guru,* which means "nature should be our teacher." The first example of this aphorism that he provided was from the Koran. Two of Adam's sons fought over their sister and one was killed. The surviving brother did not know what to do with the body until he saw two crows fighting. The surviving crow dug a hole and buried the other; the surviving brother took this crow as his guide and buried his brother. Thus, the practice of burial is both Koranic and Minangkabau adaik and has continued until the present time.

Water is a frequent subject for elaborate figures of speech. As another example of learning from nature, Datuak Rajo Panghulu offered the aphorism: "Water piped through bamboo becomes one. Decisions through discussion are unanimous." Consensus through discussion, he explained, is the democracy of the Minangkabau. Just as water is first in the earth, and then rises drawn up by the sun finally to fall as rain, so too with Indonesian and Minang democracy: the president and the panghulu are selected by the people, but then, once elevated, work for the people. Water, he continued, is essential for growing rice, for cooking, for washing; water can make electricity; water is strong. Democracy is exceedingly strong among the Minang and in the National Government. The qualities of water are our teacher: the Minang are able to learn from water and thus can create the foundation of democracy.

Several weeks after this speech I attended a Bayur wedding. The groom was from another village and consequently had to find a panghulu to act as his local representative during his wedding. (That everyone should have a panghulu to represent him on formal occasions is an axiom of Minang culture.) In explaining this situation to me, my panghulu informant cited Datuak Rajo Panghulu's statement about learning from nature and then, as illustration, presented the following traditional saying, "In perching, grasp with the claws; in flying, spring into flight." This means, he said, that when we arrive and when we leave we inform the local panghulu. We thus grasp and then release.

These figures of speech appear to be more than a convenient and pleasing way to present traditional wisdom. Rather, they suggest that nature and Minang adaik follow the same pattern. It is not just that one can learn from nature but that natural events and social form are of the same order of reality. Minangkabau life is thus congruent with natural reality. Moreover, Minang sermons often emphasize the congruence between Minang adaik and Islam by juxtaposing Minang figures of speech with an Arabic equivalent from the Koran. They thereby show the high degree of compatibility between nature, adaik, and religion.

These cases were provided by a variety of Minangkabau men whose reputations for knowledge about adaik varied from average to exceptional. I think that most members of Western culture who make and appraise explicit interpretations would find the Minang exceptional, not because they also explicitly interpret their culture, but because they interpret it so much. Even more troubling to the Western interpreter than the quantity of Minang interpretation is the nature of that interpretation. Not only is suspicion of particular Minangkabau interpretations aroused by the suggestion that everything has meaning, but this suspicion is fed by the fact that most of the responses Minang produce about the meaning of adaik seem to be contrived on the spot and, as such, idiosyncratic and unsystematic.[1]

Experience in Western culture tends to be so complex as often to appear largely random and chaotic. To understand what is going on in any sort of general way is, I think, recognized by most members of Western culture as very difficult. What patterns may exist must be sufficiently removed from the extreme complexity of experienced reality as to be discerned, if at all, only through strenuous intellectual effort.[2] Much Minang interpretation—whether by expert or not—is of appearance, of what seems to be surface and hence superficial characteristics; Minang simply do not probe deeply enough to make their explanations convincing to most members of our culture. Indeed, I have difficulty in convincing undergraduate students that Minang explanations are even intended to be explanations.

It is very much worth noting, however, that, because members of Western culture have difficulty in making much sense of the complexity of contemporary Western life, they very often may hazard no interpretation at all. Because so much of our experience is seen as random and chaotic, we may frequently accept it as indeed largely inexplicable. For instance, we rarely would even bother to think about how many spires a building happened to have. If we were pressed, we might well support our perception of randomness by suggesting that the number of spires was a historical accident. Perhaps if pressed further, we might add that while this particular architectural form may have had interpretable meaning someplace else, or at some other time, it has become for us simply a meaningless survival. Thus, when I discuss Western standards of explanation, I am referring to cases in which an explanation is in

1. I am not suggesting that Minang interpretations are unsystematic in any absolute sense. They all take place within the general context of meaning of Minang culture, which is itself, as I am trying to demonstrate, fundamentally consistent.

2. Sontag's discussion (1970) of what has become a characteristically Western approach to art provides further and similar examples of the Western style of interpretation that I am describing here.

fact produced rather than to those cases in which a phenomenon is regarded as simply a historical accident or otherwise without significance. One of the differences, then, between our standards of explanation and those of the Minang is that we explain less frequently but more thoroughly, while they explain more frequently but less thoroughly.

On further examination, other differences appear between the kinds of interpretations Minang and we are likely to produce. For instance, the reasons given for the new meaning of one of the mosque towers, for the five sides of the kaban, and for the use of unhusked rice at a house-raising clearly were based on conscious manipulation of meaning. That the meaning should be so consciously held and so readily manipulated does not correspond well to the Western concept of symbol, which holds that the connection between a symbol and its meaning is, on one hand, not initially apparent and, on the other, intrinsic. Turner (1967, p. 26), cited earlier, expresses this idea by presenting Jung's definition of a symbol as "the *best possible* expression of a *relatively unknown* fact." (The first three emphases are mine.)

In Western thought the link between symbol and its meaning is at least relatively determined and hence, if not immutable, resistant to drastic change; furthermore, the meaning of a particular symbol and the occasions of its appearance are also determined by its role in a system of symbols—by its relationship to other symbols. Hence, for the structuralist analyzing a myth or set of myths, a Freudian analyzing a personality or a literary piece, a Marxist analyzing a political/economic system, the meaning of any particular symbol is constrained by the meaning of other symbols.

Moreover, as a correlate of the Western view which regards symbols as referring to something that is "relatively unknown," the reason that symbols exist at all is because they can make possible at least oblique recognition of that which would resist direct understanding. (See Langer's discussion of presentational symbolism; Langer 1942.) Thus, not only are symbols partially shielded from consciousness and hence from conscious manipulation, but they should in this view transfer meaning from known to relatively unknown, resulting in clarification of the unknown.

Such a transfer of meaning is not apparent in the examples I have presented. Little more is understood about either the mosque towers or the community categories through having the first depict the second, except perhaps that the mosque is a central and unifying institution in the village. But this is something everyone knows anyway and is also demonstrated every Friday at the noonday service. Nor is much learned from etymology about the use and meaning of the carano and lalamak (brass urn and decorated cloth) that is not already known. Some small meaning is perhaps conveyed or generated simply through having various aspects of village life occasionally singled out for attention, as they were in these interpretations and in the representations themselves. But that meaning does not seem significantly enriched, enhanced, or augmented through its attachment to certain artifacts because the connection between meaning and vehicle is tenuous: if the mosque had had only three towers or none at all, a meaning could still have been found for it, and, conversely, the mosque is hardly the only way that community categories could be (and are) represented. Most of what was said at the Bayur panghulu meeting, both by Datuak Rajo Panghulu and by those cited in my various examples, was either already known by most Minang or, if new to them, scarcely novel. Datuak Rajo Panghulu's speech added the names of some primeval panghulu to Bayur's collective store of information about adaik; Sutan Zara Endah's etymology of carano and lalamak perhaps did the same. The meaning expressed is not hidden, obscure, opaque, or esoteric, despite the fact that not everyone may know or agree, for instance, why unhusked rather than husked rice is brought to a house-raising.

Thus, Minang interpretations appear to the Westerner to be not only superficial and vague but also arbitrary and piecemeal. Because they so easily account for everything, they never really seem to account satisfactorily for anything in particular.

What, then, is the point of these interpretations? At the very least, they convey a recognition of the ubiquity of form and hence assert that adaik is pervasive and that the Minangkabau world is characterized by order. Moreover, interpretation per se substantiates the premise that everything in adaik has meaning. Sutan Zara Endah was sure that the five sides of the packet had a meaning and on another occasion directly stated that everything had meaning. This premise was also strongly implied by the remarkable breadth of subject matter covered in Datuak Rajo Panghulu's speech and by the willingness of most Minang men to strain if necessary to provide some answer to any question that I happened to ask them about what any specific aspect of Minang life meant. (Other Western observers of the Minang have reported similar experiences to me.)

By asserting that everything has meaning and by showing that this meaning is overt and evident, the Minang were asserting the commonsense rightness of their experience as Minang: to be a reasonable person is to be a Minangkabau. They were asserting that adaik prescribes behavior and beliefs that are supremely reasonable, that are fully consonant with natural and social reality. These interpretations suggested nothing that would cause the Minang to reappraise themselves as Minang. Instead, through the public recitations as well as the informal interpretations of daily life, confirmation of the rightness of their present life came in a steady flow. In these interpretations, the Minang were not trying to point to the relatively unknown, to systematize experience, or to convey anything other than the everyday commonsense experience of their world.

Minang interpretations of adaik should not be regarded as interpretations of symbols; rather than view one of the mosque towers as a symbol of the women's organization, it would be more accurate to view it as a sign of that organization, and, in a more general sense, as an illustration of the premise that everything has meaning. Although the Minang, as I will argue in Part 4, do occasionally confront the grounds of their being, that is, probe the limits of their experience, what they say about themselves is conveyed by signs rather than symbols.

But why is so much of Minangkabau meaning conveyed by signs? Signs do not need to present, create, encompass, or reveal truth, but only to illustrate truth. Because signs are only illustrations of truth rather than the truth itself, they can be ad hoc and nonsystematic, and hence rather easily all-inclusive. (Signs can, of course, in fact be systematic, but only as the result of a major intellectual effort of the sort mustered by the medieval European church.) For the Minang, the mosque tower that formerly signified the indigenous police can, with little effort, signify the women's organization. It is only this imprecision—facilitated by the use of signs in the absence of a most strenuous program of rationalization—that allows everything to have meaning.

Symbols, in contrast, because of their inherent connection with what they symbolize, are less easily manipulated than signs to cover gaps in meaning when such appear; and in a complex culture with a history of extensive cultural contact, gaps are certainly bound to appear. Moreover, symbols, because of their links to the relatively unknown, are less suitable than signs to support and interpret the world of appearance, the world of actual daily commonsense experience.

Signs are more easily talked about, more easily learned. This is clearly advantageous for the Minang because much socialization takes place at a relatively late age and for that reason must be explicit. I was taught with fair ease how to behave as a Minang— at least how to observe baso basi—in very much the same way as were the newly receptive youth returning from abroad. (Minang are explicit that such youth must be taught baso basi.) Because signs do not have "deep" meaning, they can be readily learned by everyone irrespective of the diversity of their personal experiences abroad or even in the village.

Because signs are so easily all-inclusive and so readily learned, they are very functional for the Minang under the conditions of cultural complexity and diversity that they experience. Moreover, signs are, for them, eminently inviting since, as illustrations of truth, they promise that truth does indeed exist. Signs appear to convey portions of truth and hence collectively create an umbrella of meaning—of seeming plausibility—under which all Minang, irrespective of diversity of experience, can be brought. By only illustrating truth (or perhaps, more accurately, illustrating that there is truth) signs manage to avoid the burden of demonstrating what that truth actually is and that it actually exists. Signs thus promise more than they actually deliver, but it is the promise that counts.

In the Minangkabau case, the truth which their signs promise through illustration is that adaik is inherently true. Since, Islam aside, adaik encompasses everything that is right and proper for a Minangkabau, anything that is right and proper for a Minang-kabau is an illustration of the validity and comprehensiveness of adaik. For this illustration, it does not really matter whether the mosque has four towers or three and whether these towers stand for the four village groups or, perhaps, the three cords of Minang society.

For the Minang, that there is truth never comes into question, and the only problems in discerning the meaning of a custom come in deciding what aspect of truth that particular custom illustrates. (For the Westerner, truth itself is almost always in question, and argument must first attempt to establish that truth before convincing illustrations of it can be presented.)

If meaning for the Minang is not at a great remove from ap-pearance, and if almost any interpretation illustrates the idea that appearance and daily experience do have meaning, the question still remains as to why these particular kinds of interpretations of appearance are favored. There are, in actuality, certain areas of Minang life that need clarification.

Minang do not, as I have indicated, believe that their social life should be static; rather, as Abdullah (1971, 1972) has noted and I subsequently confirmed by my own fieldwork, Minangkabau strongly believe that their world must expand and develop if it is to fulfill its potential for perfection. A crucial problem for them is to regulate this change so that the distinctively Minangkabau—right and proper—characteristics will be preserved. This is a di-lemma faced by individuals as they return from abroad to the home village; and this is also a dilemma faced by the home village collectively, as it tries to require a life in accord with basic Minang patterns and values while responding to pressures for change and development from the encroaching external world. It is my con-clusion that the continual interpretation of adaik is necessary not only to confirm that forms, meaning, and truth exist, but also to help the community make judgments which allow both continuity and development in their adaik.

Most of the relatively unfamiliar information that emerges in discussions about adaik concerns the origins of particular aspects of Minang adaik. Such knowledge would include the stray facts of the sort that Datuak Rajo Panghulu presented, such as the names of the most primeval panghulu, the original meaning of "Datuak," and so on. The ability to present etymologies is valued because, in stating the origin of the names of adaik practices, the origin of those practices themselves is also presented. The implicit claim is made, in showing the origins of well-established current practices, that these are also the original—the *usali*—Minangkabau practices themselves. Since, virtually by definition, the original Minang practices are right and proper, such interpretations validate existing practice.

To know and value the original forms of adaik also facilitates appraising social change and, possibly, controlling the form of that change, or at least justifying that change if it is inevitable. The Minang explicitly distinguish between two types of adaik. One is called *cupak usali* (the original measure) and is not subject to change, either because it embodies natural law or quintessential Minang custom. The other type of adaik, called *cupak buatan* (the constructed measure) includes particular manifestations of the more fundamental, more general, cupak usali. Cupak buatan is subject to change through consensus, provided that change does not contradict or threaten the core cupak usali. I heard again and again, in Minang discussions of particular examples of change, that the intent of the original and essential practice—the cupak usali—was preserved. Not just the original form but the original purpose of the cupak usali is often clarified through a statement of origins: the purported etymologies of *carano* and *lalamak* are, for example, statements of original intent. Interpretation or clarification of adaik shows what the purpose of that aspect of adaik is: the interpretation of why unhusked rather than husked rice is brought to a house-raising is a statement of the intent, the purpose, of such a gift. By discerning the purpose in the original pattern, and that in the present or proposed pattern, it may consequently be possible to show congruity between them: the mosque tower can be shown still to illustrate the principal categories of the community, despite the substitution of the women's group for the indigenous police force.

Minang take pride in the flexibility of the adaik, a flexibility given expression in such proverbs as "When the flood comes the bathing place changes." All discussions of the social changes with which the Minang feel comfortable follow this same conservative mode of interpretation. Another homey and typical example is that formerly one traveled abroad on foot and now one goes by bus. Or to use Datuak Rajo Panghulu's variant of this: formerly one went by sailing boat to Jakarta but now one goes by steamship. In such interpretations current Minang practices which obviously differ in form from original and core practices are seen as maintaining the intent, and hence the validity, of those original practices.

If interpretation mainly consists in clarifying the original intent of adaik practices to show that there has been continuity of that intent, what constitutes a convincing clarification? As the examples amply show, considerable disparity of interpretation exists. Yet informants vehemently denied my suggestion that, because there was so much disagreement on the meaning of particular signs, interpretation was therefore just a matter of opinion. There is, I was told, one and only one right answer (another way of stating that truth exists). In response to my question as to how one recognizes which of all these conflicting answers is the right one, I was told to ask someone who was an expert. And who decides who is an expert? The community decides, came the reply.

What, then, are the marks of an expert? And what distinguishes a merely competent older man or a local expert from someone of major reputation like Datuak Rajo Panghulu in the way each interprets adaik?

Chapter 5
The Expert

An expert has three distinguishing qualities: knowledge of adaik, exceptional intelligence, and the confidence—the "bearing"—that follows from knowledge and intelligence.

When I asked how particular individuals in Bayur had gained their knowledge of adaik, I was told that they had learned what they knew from having extensive experience in the community, observing Minang life as it was lived, from holding conversations with knowledgeable peers and seniors, and, perhaps, from reading books about adaik written by men like Idroes Hakimi Datuak Rajo Panghulu and M. Rasjid Manggis Datuak Radjo Panghoeloe. One local man who aspired to be an expert had copied by hand a book on Minangkabau adaik to which he referred frequently and openly to substantiate his interpretations; another had a little notebook in which he recorded for future reference the various odd pieces of Minang lore that came his way, including some excerpts from Datuak Rajo Panghulu's speech; yet another owned and consulted a very old book about Minang customs. These men frequently mentioned to each other, to anyone else listening in the coffee shop, and to me, bits of information concerning, for instance, the origin of certain Minang terms, the names of early Minang rajas, and the ethnic and cultural origins of the Minang. Much of this information had apparently been recently acquired, usually from their readings.

There were obviously various grades of experts. When I asked what made one man more expert than another, I was told it had something to do with mental endowment, with a high IQ. (That was the term used.) There were men in Bayur who were considered experts because they knew quantitatively more than most of the others. But, significantly, they were not regarded as being as expert as someone like Sutan Zara Endah who, because of his superior intelligence, could do more than just present the facts and interpretations which he had heard or read. He could develop and defend his own interpretations of adaik.

Beyond the local level there was Datuak Rajo Panghulu. He was patently among the most expert of experts. His knowledge was vast and he was obviously able to think clearly and quickly, and, for his audience, convincingly about adaik. To illustrate: at the end of his talk he called for questions. These did not challenge or indicate skepticism about what he had said but were requests that he clarify aphorisms, frequently ones he had not used in his speech. One such puzzling aphorism translates as "The panghulu cuts sharply and quickly with his sword through the throat of his matrilineal junior." Datuak Rajo Panghulu had not heard this expression before but suggested that it had the following meaning: a sword is made from steel, has the quality of creating fear, and thus serves to control and direct. The sword is sharp and this means that the thought, sight, and everything else about the panghulu should be sharp. Because of the fear of the panghulu's sharpness, his matrilineal junior would accept his direction. This aphorism, he concluded, indicates that a characteristic of the panghulu is to impose discipline.

Finally, confidence—the bearing of an authority—has its effect on a man's reputation as an expert. Sutan Zara Endah and Datuak Rajo Panghulu were eloquent, full of confidence, authoritative. Sutan Zara Endah stressed that whereas others in the village might give me just any answer that came to them, he would tell me only the truth.

In part to test Sutan Zara Endah's reputation as an expert, I asked him a long list of questions concerning aspects of adaik which had puzzled others or had provoked them into what seemed to me especially weak explanations. He dealt easily and often ingeniously with all of these except one. The only question that did puzzle him at this (or any other) time concerned the five sides of the ceremonial packet, but, as previously mentioned, he soon provided an answer. He was able to talk much more analytically than anyone else in the village about the characteristics of adaik. During this conversation, he said, for example, that the various numbered lists so important in Minang adaik were the "synthesis" (his word) of Hindu, Greek, and Islamic philosophical traditions. The number four (e.g., four kinds of speech) reflected the Greek influence; three (e.g., three cords) reflected Hindu influence; five (e.g., five duties of a Muslim) reflected Islamic influence.

Sutan Zara Endah also volunteered a great number of interpretations, many of which he regarded as distinctive. The word *Minangkabau* does not mean "victorious water buffalo," as everyone else thought, but originally was *minang kabu,* meaning "native land."[1] Both my assistant and I immediately questioned him about the traditional form of the Minangkabau roof, because its upswept ends were usually said to follow the curve of the victorious water buffalo's horns. Sutan Zara Endah replied that this curve of the roof did indeed follow the curve of a water buffalo's horns, but not because of any reference to the victorious water buffalo legend. It was because the water buffalo's qualities of strength, patience, and usefulness characterize the Minangkabau people.

My assistant and I in a later conversation agreed that no one else considered these qualities, especially patience, to be particularly characteristic of the Minang. Sutan Zara Endah, out of an interest in providing a distinctive interpretation, disrupted one of the few existing generally accepted sets of congruencies of interpretation, that relating the name of the Minangkabau, their house form, and their legendary victorious buffalo. Thus, despite his superior resourcefulness in defending his interpretations, Sutan

1. The widely accepted derivation of *Minangkabau* as victorious water buffalo refers to a legendary battle between the Minangkabau and the Javanese. The Javanese placed as their representative on the field of battle a formidable female water buffalo. The Minang countered with a not yet weaned water buffalo calf on whose head they affixed iron spikes. The calf ducked under the cow to nurse, and in so doing impaled and killed her. The Minangkabau were thus victorious and the Javanese invaders returned home. Despite my efforts, some of which were quite direct, I could not elicit any speculation on the possible meaning of this encounter for the matrilineal Minangkabau. The only conclusion my informants drew for me was that this story showed that the Minang are much shrewder than the Javanese.

Zara Endah showed little more concern than most in making his interpretation consistent with others.

In another session with Sutan Zara Endah a few days after I had heard his view that the five sides of the ceremonial packet stood for the four types of speech plus religion, I asked him why this interpretation was preferable to, for instance, one that considered the five sides as representing the three cords (adaik, religion, and government) plus the two measures of adaik (the original and the constructed). He seemed somewhat startled by my suggestion, and immediately asked who had told me this. After I told him that it was my own interpretation, he relaxed. In the following conversational lull, I presented an analogy between a piece of ritual apparatus (called *siriah gadang*) and the five-sided packet, each of which is associated with panghulu. Just as the three cords were represented in the three tiers of the siriah gadang, so too, I suggested, the three cords might also appear as part of the meaning of the five-sided packet.

Sutan Zara Endah's response to this was easily the most sophisticated that I heard in Bayur and showed his superior analytic ability. It did, however, appear to rest on the traditional original measure and constructed measure distinction, a distinction between degrees of generality and of importance. He said that the three cords as presented in the siriah gadang were the most fundamental principles of Minang life and adaik, and therefore what was needed was a less abstract statement, a realization of these principles in practice. The four types of speech, as informed by the spirit of religion, constituted just such a manifestation in practice of these principles. To my response that I did not see why the siriah gadang and the five-sided packet could not both be on the same level of abstraction, and each have its realization in some of the myriad other representations present in the ritual, he replied that there could not be two representations for the same thing. I said that there were many representations for the Republic of Indonesia; for instance, there were the words themselves, there was Pancasila (the five principles), and there was the flag. His response was that these were all on different levels of abstraction. And that was where our discussion ended, although he was never able to say why he thought the siriah gadang was more abstract than the five-sided packet, and in fact the only reason that I could see for discussing them together had been my initial and fortuitous example. He was, however, able to muster a vigorous defense of his position, and that was one of the reasons he was considered an expert on adaik. (I was pleased to note that my suggested interpretation must have seemed plausible to the Minangkabau since, shortly afterward, the man who had associated the five sides of the packet with the three raja said that each of these raja stood for one of the cords. I assumed that he knew of my discussion with Sutan Zara Endah.)

Minang clearly recognize that wide differences exist in interpretations of particular aspects of adaik. Virtually all of the older men who aspired to be considered well versed in the meaning of adaik urged me to consult with them before recording the views of others. Several, in fact, said that I need consult only with them, since talking to others would only produce confusing and wrong answers. All of these men strongly warned me against asking and recording the views of youth. Not only are youth insufficiently versed in adaik to behave in an entirely orderly way, they simply do not have detailed knowledge about its origins. Everyone I talked to on the subject indicated that there was only one right answer to what some aspect of adaik meant, and that it was important to them that I record the right answer in my description of Bayur's adaik.

Diversity of interpretation itself did not seriously trouble my informants, even when diverse interpretations were advanced by men of some reputation rather than by youth. Indeed, they rejected my suggestion that if experts disagreed there might be no way to differentiate among their rival interpretations.

Once, for instance, when I was typing in my office, Sutan Zara Endah came in, apparently to impart more adaik. He began by saying that there were only four reasons that ancestral property could be pawned. I countered by saying that there was no agreement on what these four reasons were, cited some of the divergent opinion current in Bayur, and also mentioned a list made in the 1920s which gave six reasons. He specifically challenged this, arguing that three and four are numbers important to the Minangkabau and that therefore a list of six was not likely to be correct. He was only initially troubled that not all *authorities* agreed on these reasons. He recovered quickly and pointed out that this disagreement was superficial: all lists conveyed the same fundamental and traditional intent of conserving property; moreover, everyone in the community would agree that such property should be pawned or sold only in the most dire need.

The idea that everyone in the community would agree that matrilineal property should be conserved leads back to the central theme of Minangkabau experience. The community is ultimate judge as to the correctness of all aspects of life: the community is the final arbiter not only of daily conduct but of truth and meaning. The experts propose interpretations, but the community has the last word on the validity of those interpretations: the community is virtually the ultimate repository of truth about adaik. Minangkabau very frequently talk about the importance of reaching consensus through discussion in community life. Datuak Rajo Panghulu used the word *mupakaik* (consensus) and a more modern expression *democrasi* many times in his speech, and also cited several aphorisms about the nature of consensus. One, already mentioned, is that as water piped through bamboo becomes one, decisions through discussion are unanimous. Another is that as flame lives in a cooking fire made from crossed pieces of wood, so consensus and truth result from the give-and-take of discussion.

Subject to some qualification, Minang believe that if truth (of the sort with which humans rather than Allah are concerned) does not actually lie on the surface, it does lie rather close to that surface: it can be discerned or uncovered by discussion and, once revealed, will be immediately recognizable to all as truth. It is a characteristic Minangkabau habit while explaining something to make a few largely descriptive observations and then to lean back, smile, and say "Ah." This suggests that all is now clear when, at least to the Western observer, the question seems to have been only broached. The Minang term for this capacity of quick comprehension is *raso jo pareso*. This capacity rests on a sense of compatability, the perception that an interpretation or figure of speech fits comfortably—*cocok*—with an established sense of what the world is like. The community accepts—*tarimo*—that which it can perceive to be compatible with its sense of the world, whether it is the wisdom of Datuak Rajo Panghulu, the interpretations of local adaik experts, or the conduct of individuals, perhaps fresh from abroad. The perception of truth—based on the sense of the fit characterized as cocok—is essentially an aesthetic reaction.

The aspect of one of my extended sessions with Sutan Zara Endah that proved most interesting to Jhon was Sutan Zara Endah's comment that the traditional Minang histories which trace Minang descent from Alexander the Great are incorrect. On the contrary, Sutan Zara Endah said, the historical origins of the Minang lay in Indochina, not Greece. The Minang claim kinship with Alexander simply because he was great. Minang, he said, are always claiming kinship with important men. Jhon's response to this indicates the process by which a man comes to be considered an expert through having his interpretations accepted by the community. Sutan Zara Endah's rejection of this tie with Alexander, based on evaluation of historical evidence acquired through his reading, was accepted as true by Jhon, essentially because of the wry and frequently made observation that Minang like to claim kinship with important people. Jhon repeated this point several times to me and to his friends, who also seemed to think it fit their understanding of Minang behavior.

Sutan Zara Endah's interpretations tended to be accepted, which was why he was regarded as an expert. Another schoolteacher who was also well read was not so regarded and, when discussing with others the differences between these two, I was told that the second just expresses his own thoughts. This does not mean, as I first thought, that individuals should not think about adaik. It meant in this case, rather, that no one else agrees with this second schoolteacher—the community does not accept his views. There was not, of course, unanimity in these matters: the second schoolteacher did have some supporters, and not all of what Sutan Zara Endah said about adaik was accepted or even regarded as of much interest.

Although the community can distinguish a true interpretation from a false one, judging from the wide range of interpretations I collected, it does not often choose to distinguish. I was probably somewhat more aware than most—certainly more so than Jhon had been—of differences in interpretations, since Minang do not go around, as I did, systematically soliciting opinion. However, when diversity of interpretation is uncovered, the reputations of those advancing different views may be sufficiently unequal that only one view really receives a hearing. But it often makes small difference if a selection cannot be easily made between conflicting views. Many Minang interpretations have slight implication for action. The derivation of the terms *carano* and *lalamak* (the brass urn and decorated cloth), the significance of the mosque towers, and so on, will not affect how decisions are made and behavior appraised.

For this reason, despite assertions that there is only one right meaning, and that the community is the ultimate judge of that meaning, many aspects of adaik never acquire a single standardized meaning. It is much more important for the Minang that there be too much meaning rather than too little. An abundance of interpretation supports their fundamental proposition that everything has meaning.

Furthermore, an abundance of meaning suggests that the pursuit of this meaning is relatively open to anyone. Although a Minang village has panghulu who conform more closely in their behavior to the ideal patterns of adaik than most, and has experts on adaik who display a greater understanding of adaik than most, nonetheless adaik, both as a context of behavior and of meaning, is for everyone. For the Minang it is supremely reasonable to be a Minang, which is one of the reasons, I think, that Minang remain loyal Minang even after, in some cases, years spent abroad. All of their interpretations of adaik suggest the reasonability of that adaik. Because of that reasonability, the community can judge—accepting or not—particular interpretations, and for the same reason individual members of the community can form their own interpretations to try out on the rest of the community. Anyone so inclined can think about the difference between husked and unhusked rice at a house-raising.

To be a Minang is to move with reality itself. Many of the Minang figures of speech, such as those about birds alighting and Minang checking in with their panghulu, water evaporating and Minang governance, suggest that things are what they are and do what they do. A similar sort of literal, commonsense view of reality is shown in the belief that reality actually holds four, and only four, types of speech. Although individuals may disagree as to which of several interpretations is true, the idea that there is a true, sensible interpretation is not at issue. Agreement, although perhaps desirable, is not essential, because the style of interpretation itself demonstrates that Minang life is supremely reasonable: morality and reality, aesthetics and ethics, are in accord.

The style of interpretation favored by Minangkabau society is the same both for the interpretation of persons and of society: it follows in both cases a sign-oriented aesthetic.[2] Baso basi is seen as a sign of respect for others, as a sign that constraint is accepted, and as a sign that an individual is willing to live within the community. In other words, it is a sign that an individual is willing to conform to adaik. What little interpretation of motivation there is tends to be according to a standard and limited inventory of signs or illustrations of generally recognized human nature. The reasons offered to explain why someone goes mad are similar in lack of specificity to those offered to explain why the mosque tower means one thing rather than another. In one case, interpretation consists in stating something thought to be true of human nature in general—individuals may go mad if they worry too much about money. In the other, interpretation consists in stating something else thought to be true about nature or adaik—that birds alight, and the Minangkabau village once had a police force or now has a women's organization. In both cases, whether the interpretation is of persons or society, and whether that interpretation proceeds by linking the general to the specific or the specific to the specific, there is an absence of any essential and fundamental connection between behavior, custom, artifact, and its ascribed meaning. In both cases there is no interest in probing for any hidden connections that are not part of, or close to, immediate experience.

This is not to deny that the relatively apparent may require interpretation and that such interpretation may require ingenuity. Minang do find aspects of their experience puzzling: questions such as What does an expensive gift to a Western anthropologist mean?

2. What little information I have suggests that Minang also approach their art with a sign-oriented aesthetic. Most paintings I saw were largely realistic portraits. One depicted a man with staring eyes, an indication of his magical power. One painting was a rendering of a particular scene in a traditional story. A Minang woodcarver explained his designs to me as conveying particular Minang aphorisms: each part of the design was a stylization of a specific referent.

What does the five-sided packet mean? have already been presented. Questions such as What do the particular number and variety of feast foods at a wedding indicate about the sentiments of the family of the bride toward the family of the groom? could be added. (See Prindiville 1979 for a discussion of communication through food.) Minang may find aspects of these experiences puzzling at first, but they are unlikely to find them persistently baffling because the parameters and elements of interpretation are largely evident. And they are largely evident irrespective of their degree of generality: the characteristics of human nature, including the reasons humans go mad, the number of types of speech inherent in reality, the qualities of unhusked rice, and the names of the village groups are (or easily could be) well known and part of everyday Minang experience. The interpretation Minang engage in consists not in cracking a code but in deciphering a message—which may of course contain ambiguous and poorly formed phrases, to say nothing of misspellings—presented in an idiom that is well understood and is part of daily experience.

It is possible to subscribe to the view, held by most if not all symbolic anthropologists, that to seek and create meaning is to be human, yet still question that such meaning must run well outside of normal, daily experience. Why must "ultimate concerns" be "deep concerns"? Why must members of a culture be convinced of the rightness of their lives only by going well beyond appearances? In the West, we expect symbols to reveal rather than merely illustrate meaning, and an elusive meaning at that. The connotation of "symbol" speaks to the rootlessness of Western experience, the homelessness of Western consciousness, but not of the experience and consciousness of those whose reality is much less in question. Although adaik is difficult for the Minangkabau to talk about apart from its particular aspects, and although it is accompanied by strong emotions, this does not mean that adaik is mysterious, deep, elusive, or unknown. In Part 4 I will examine the most condensed images the Minang construct of the nature of adaik and of the nature of human beings and their potentially anarchic energy.

With the ascension of the panghulu comes a most scrupulous observance of social form. The structure of a Minang village is laid bare with a clear specification of the form of kin groups and the relationship of those groups to the community at large. Baso basi appears at its most extensive as part of a pervasive concern with protocol. Minangkabau themselves regard the ascension of a pan-ghulu to be the quintessence of their adaik and are preoccupied during this ceremony and its preliminaries with the need to have the various forms composing adaik correctly and fully enacted. During this time there is an overall celebration of social form, sometimes, as in the speeches, to the virtual eclipse of content.

The themes of the pig hunt—presented after the account of the ascension of the panghulu—are very different. The pig hunt is *almost* the opposite, with the emphasis laid not on depicting form but on depicting the margins of formlessness. Violence and death, assertion and exuberant physical activity, all are ingredients that make the pig hunt experience an image of energy rather than of control and form.

In the ascension of a panghulu and in the pig hunt, statements are made about reality which clearly contrast with the experience and interpretation of daily life, but the differences are more of emphasis than of kind.

PART IV
THE ENACTMENT OF FORM

Chapter 6
Adaik Incarnate

Minang regard the ascension of a man to the panghulu title of his matrilineage as the most important of adaik ceremonies. On this occasion, they display adaik in a form so concentrated that it virtually becomes distilled. In so doing, they not only display life fully ordered in accord with the particular social forms of adaik, but at the same time provide a commentary on the nature of social form itself. This ceremony of exemplification and concentration focuses on those individuals whose normal lives within the community most exemplify and concentrate adaik. The ceremony of ascension to clan title shows the most constrained of the community, the panghulu, at their most constrained. The quintessence of adaik is thus portrayed: the nature of social form—social order—is displayed with axiomatic clarity.

These ceremonies of ascension take place infrequently, since until very recently a panghulu usually held his position for life, or at least until beset by the feebleness of advanced age. During my fieldwork, however, the title of Datuak Bandaro did fall vacant and I was able to examine the entire process of replacement of a panghulu. The Minang themselves regard this process as falling into three stages: selection of the candidate, preliminary ceremonial arrangements, and the ceremony of ascension itself. There is, as I shall show in this chapter, throughout all three of these stages an emphasis on order as expressed in the themes of personal constraint and cultural continuity, with a concordant suppression of themes of personal freedom and cultural change.

In the selection of the candidate, the role of individual choice, and so of private political interests within the matrilineage, is greatly limited. Nor is innovation in standards of procedure encouraged. Individuals do not actively contend for title. All are measured against the same relatively fixed and traditional standards of competence. Moreover, there is a meticulous adherence to an adaik procedure that limits eligibility for the title to a particular matrilineal group at a given time. Thus, choice is so constrained by the existence of fixed standards and procedure that there is minimal latitude for an individual to attempt to maximize his own political interests through support of someone in particular.

In the preliminary ceremonial arrangements there is also a suppression of private or sectional interests in favor of the concerns of the larger group, in this case the community as a whole. Although the panghulu does represent a particular matrilineage, he is nonetheless seen in this part of the ceremonial sequence, as well as in the eventual exercise of his duties, to be a figure who embodies public interests, someone whose responsibility is to uphold adaik in the community at large.

Within the ceremony of ascension itself is the continuation of the pattern of order achieved through constraint and continuity. Here social form frequently takes precedence over content. Individuality—as well as private and sectional interests more generally—is submerged, and indeed virtually extinguished, through mutual adherence to the constraint of traditional social forms.

Thus, at a time when an individual is ascending to power and his matrilineal group is the center of community attention, there is a consistent effort to minimize the formation and expression of narrow and divisive political interests. The selection procedure does not favor the development of political divisions within the matrilineal group. The preliminary ceremonial arrangements minimize the political opposition between the members of the sponsoring matrilineage and the other members of the community. Finally, in the ceremony of ascension itself, there is the final diminution of particular political interests when a resolution of the tension between individuals and their social forms occurs. At this point, individuals become their social forms, they become adaik incarnate. This provides the clearest expression a group of Minang can experience of themselves composing an ordered community living according to adaik.

SELECTION OF THE CANDIDATE: THE CONSTRAINT
OF INDIVIDUALITY

The Minang talked readily to me, not only on this occasion when they were looking for a new panghulu but at other times as well, about the characteristics a panghulu should have. Since a panghulu is an exemplar of conduct according to adaik, ideally he should be selected from those of the community most knowledgeable about adaik. This suggests he should have reached at least middle age; youth or even young married men are not usually disposed to make a serious study of adaik. The group within the community most interested in learning the intricacies of adaik may, however, not be especially eligible. This group is composed of the elderly, largely retired men, who often study adaik to combat the intellectual torpor of retirement in the village, and the insecurity and embarrassment of being largely nonproductive urang sumando. These men, despite their knowledge and free time, are for two reasons often not considered as prospective panghulu: they do not have the financial means and they are not sufficiently impressive as persons.

A panghulu, if not rich, should at least have adequate resources to help his *anak buah*—those under his authority—if need be, and to pay for a major portion of the expensive ceremony of ascension to the panghulu title. What is even more important, though, especially at the present time, is that a panghulu should be able to make his anak buah afraid of him; otherwise, youth in particular may simply ignore what he says.

There was general agreement that Datuak Batuah and Datuak Tamajo Basa were the most effective panghulu in Bayur. Both were knowledgeable about adaik and had adequate means. Both were physically vigorous and, in addition, formidably versed in magic. In contrast, an older panghulu who was somewhat deficient in all of these attributes often elicited scarcely veiled contempt rather than respect. This man complained bitterly to me several times that being a panghulu had become thankless because adaik, religion, and government, the three cords binding together the Minangkabau world, no longer were the only forces strongly pulling on the people of Bayur. Although I doubt that he would have been regarded as a very effective panghulu in an earlier era, most people would have agreed with him that the youth were less likely to defer to their panghulu than formerly. As the attention of village youth was increasingly focused on the attractions of life abroad, a village panghulu remained effective only if he could compel respect because of his personal formidability.

The people of Bayur see the forces of the outside world as currently affecting the role of the panghulu in several other ways as well. Because the village economy is weak, those panghulu who are not retired often have to work at a variety of enterprises to make ends meet. The panghulu mentioned earlier, who worked simultaneously in Bayur as photographer, tailor, and rice farmer, was typical. As a consequence, these men are thought to be too busy making their own livings to inquire weekly at the house of each of their anak buah to see if everything is all right, as they are said to have done in the past. However, although they are less intimately involved in the lives of their matrilineal charges, they still do come, as has been indicated, to adjudicate land disputes, settle quarrels, and so forth. Indeed, this aspect of their role has remained of such importance that I was told emphatically that life was feasible for the increasing numbers of Minang abroad only because they knew that their panghulu was looking after the interests of their kin at home in times of crisis.

However, the same economic factors which lead greater numbers of Minang to stay abroad, and thus to rely more heavily on their panghulu to provide guidance for those at home, also make it increasingly difficult for the panghulu to provide this service. Since panghulu face the same economic problems as everyone else, they too have been increasingly likely to be abroad. Bayur has attempted to cope with the problems created by absentee panghulu in two ways. According to adaik, each panghulu has an assistant (wakia) and designated successor. Of late, this assistant panghulu has been increasingly likely to stand in for the panghulu while the latter is abroad. However, since the assistant panghulu himself has been often abroad, the panghulu's matrilineage found itself frequently forced to select an informal replacement.

These arrangements for substitution have come to be regarded as often too haphazard and confusing, and several years before my study the Bayur panghulu—that is, those in residence—collectively decided that a panghulu who had been abroad and thus largely absent from Bayur for over two years must relinquish the title to someone who can look after the resident anak buah directly.

So not only should a prospective panghulu be knowledgeable about adaik, of adequate means, and personally formidable, he should also actually live in Bayur. Such individuals, the people of Bayur were coming to realize, are not easy to find. The reason, indeed, there was a search during the time of my study for a man to assume the panghulu title of Datuak Bandaro was because this position had just been relinquished in response to the new residence policy by a man living abroad. The search for his successor was greatly complicated by the fact that most of those qualified to serve also lived abroad.

The village of Bayur follows the more democratic of the two Minangkabau political traditions. This means, in part, that the panghulu title rotates according to a prescribed pattern among a set of related matrilineal groups, rather than residing permanently in a single and most senior line. Consequently, once the letter of resignation was received in Bayur, the search for the next occupant of the title of Datuak Bandaro was conducted in the matrilineal group whose turn had come in the pattern of rotation. At the same time the group at one further remove in the line of rotation met to select the man who would become Datuak Marahun, the assistant panghulu to Datuak Bandaro, and who would, in the normal course of events, ultimately become Datuak Bandaro himself. (As one of a number of complicating circumstances in this particular case, the assistant panghulu to Datuak Bandaro had resigned just before the title was relinquished from abroad, and so there was no previously selected successor available.)

One of the consequences of a panghulu title changing hands is that matrilineal kinship groups receive their clearest definition. Within the matriclan itself—the suku—the composition and relationship of the lesser matrilineal units become clarified as people review and follow the selection procedure. Moreover, as we shall see, social morphology becomes further clarified within the village as groups related to the candidate in various ways assume different sorts of roles in the financing and organizing of the ceremony of ascension itself.

In Bayur the most fundamental matrilineal kinship group is the *turunan*, a property-holding group of at most three generations. The next largest is the *periuak*, at most six generations deep. In such a group usually only members of the senior generation claim to know the name of the apical female. A cluster of periuak form a *payuang*, and it is this payuang which holds a panghulu title. All the members of this payuang are regarded and referred to as the matrilineal kin and the responsibility—the anak buah—of their panghulu. Just as a group of periuak form a payuang, a group of payuang are linked together to form the largest unit of kinship, the suku. Each of the six suku in Bayur, but not in all Minang villages, is exogamous. Members of a suku postulate common matrilineal descent, although no one pretends to know the genealogies of any groups larger than the periuak. Finally, there are often several payuang within a suku which are thought—without the possibility of demonstration—to be more closely related than others. Such linked payuang are called a *jinjinan* (literally, a branch).

Datuak Bandaro is a title belonging to the Piliang suku. The selection of a candidate to fill this position was of general interest to all the members of this entire matriclan, since he would, along with the others, represent the suku as a whole. However, the group most involved in providing a new Datuak Bandaro was the payuang which he would supervise. Within this payuang, the members of the periuak whose turn in the rotation had come were yet more vitally concerned in finding an acceptable candidate. These periuak members were particularly discomfited to realize just how little choice they had. The males of their periuak who were actually living in Bayur and who thus met the new requirement were either so old as to be feeble or were still in school as teenagers or children. All of the mature males who had reasonable knowledge of adaik, wealth, and formidability were away, and all of these, with one exception, lived well beyond the boundaries of West Sumatra. The one exception became the candidate. His name was Firdaus and he was a thirty-two-year-old army lieutenant stationed a hundred miles away in Padang, the provincial capital. As I well remembered, this city was some six hours distant by bus.

The members of the Piliang suku I talked to were distressed, as the irony of having to replace an absentee panghulu with another absentee panghulu did not escape them. They stressed, however, that although Firdaus was not actually living in Bayur, he would be able to visit with more ease than had the previous Datuak Bandaro. However, the assistant and successor to Datuak Bandaro had been selected from those currently living in Bayur. The new Datuak Marahun was a man named Samsul Bahri, and although the field of contenders from the appropriate periuak had been comparably limited, he was actually in residence. He could, then, as Datuak Marahun, assume some of the duties of Datuak Bandaro while Firdaus was away.

Nor did anyone claim that Firdaus was particularly well qualified in other respects. The most that any Piliang seemed willing to argue was that, with help, Firdaus might be adequate. Although young and certainly not celebrated for his knowledge of adaik, he seemed eager to learn and had promised to seek the advice of other panghulu before acting in adaik matters. Although his army pay would not stretch much beyond supporting his wife and their two children in Padang, he had managed to send some money home to his mother in Bayur to pay a portion of the expenses for the ceremony of his ascension. Moreover, others, particularly in his periuak, had offered to help pay for the ceremony. Although little more than a youth himself, his experience as an army officer might give him a sufficient air of formidability to cause local youth to respect his authority. In any case, Firdaus was their only potentially credible candidate.

Obvious throughout this process of selecting the Datuak Bandaro was the importance to the members of this payuang that there in fact be a Datuak Bandaro. Moreover, the members of this payuang were steadfast in following precisely the complicated procedure as specified by adaik in their selection of their new exemplar of adaik. The pattern of rotation was followed, despite its complexity and the fact that it did not yield an ideal candidate. Although people were aware that the payuang contained individuals who were better qualified to act as a panghulu than Firdaus, there was no suggestion that the pattern of rotation be abandoned or altered to accommodate a more favorable choice. (If the appropriate periuak could not have found an adequate candidate, they could have relinquished their turn, and the choice would then be up to the next periuak in line.)

In their scrupulous adherence to procedure is a statement of the extreme importance of social form itself. The process of selection is highly ordered and thus relatively immune to the vagaries of individual interests and preferences.

PRELIMINARY CEREMONIAL ARRANGEMENT: THE BALANCING OF THE PAROCHIAL AND THE PUBLIC

Because it is important to all inhabitants of Bayur that they regard themselves as a community living according to adaik, it is a source of general civic concern when a panghulu title falls open and of general civic pride when the community is able to proclaim once again that all of its forty-four titles are filled. The ascension of a man to a panghulu title is of considerable importance, for other reasons too, not only within that payuang and suku, but within the community at large. Although panghulu are primarily responsible for guiding their anak buah, they do represent their anak buah in conflicts with members of other kin groups. Furthermore, some of the panghulu are members of a group that advises the mayor, and all of them compose a council concerned with adaik, its interpretation and practice.

Preliminary ceremonial arrangements for the ascension to office indeed reflect both the parochial and the public nature of the panghulu's role.

Once the candidate is selected, his periuak meets with only a smattering of others to make preliminary plans at what is called the small meeting (*baduduak ketek*.) This is followed a few days later by an expanded meeting, the large meeting (*baduduak gadang*), to which the entire payuang, associated urang sumando, plus a few interested outsiders, are invited. These interested outsiders are in a sense representative of the community as a whole. At this second meeting, resources in money and manpower are appraised and individuals are selected to fill key roles. A decision must be made concerning whether the ascension ceremony should consist only of the basic *ambalau* (to fit in place) or whether the ambalau should be followed by the more elaborate *baralek panghulu* (installation of the panghulu). With the ambalau, adaik is satisfied

relatively inexpensively and installation in office is complete. However, if the sponsoring periuak is sufficiently ambitious, wealthy,
and energetic, it may also commit itself to yet another day of
ceremony, parade, and feasting with the baralek panghulu. This
is the grandest ceremony the Minang have, and is a source of
lasting prestige to the panghulu and his anak buah.

During their second meeting, Firdaus and his periuak did in
fact announce that a baralek panghulu would be given. The main
subsequent business of the meeting was to select the men and
women from the community at large who would have specialized
ceremonial roles: four women—referred to as the Four Women—
were required by adaik to collect and arrange ritual paraphernalia
and to supervise the preparation and serving of food; four men—
referred to as the Four Men—were required to help greet, seat,
and serve the guests; two orators were required to present *pas-
ambahan*, that is, the archaic embellished speech of formal occasions. The schedule was set with the ambalau fixed for Saturday,
March 8, only four days hence, with the baralek to follow on the
ninth.

In anticipation of the ambalau, men would shore up the ancestral
house belonging to Firdaus's periuak so that it would not collapse
under the weight of anticipated throngs, construct an outdoor cooking shelter and make a ceremonial arch. Both men and women
would borrow or rent the plates, glasses, and cookware needed to
feed the hundreds who would attend. Moreover, Firdaus's *bako*
(members of the suku of his father) needed to organize for their
participation in the portion of the baralek panghulu called *mariak
bantiang*. For this they must hire a horse and find a small boy
willing and suitable to be perched upon it, dressed as a raja; they
must cook and then present a considerable amount of food. Horse,
boy, and food then would be conveyed in a procession for which
any of the women of Bayur who wished to parade would prepare
their ancestral finery. This and much more promised several extremely busy and correspondingly exciting days ahead.

Wednesday, March 5

While the bako began to make arrangements for the mariak bantiang, the Piliang hosts were already in the midst of activity.
By noon that Wednesday, Datuak Maleko, one of the assistant

panghulu for the Piliang hosts, who was primarily in charge of logistics, looked frazzled but happy. He said that he and the Four Women had begun to assemble cushions, carpets, decorated cloths, brass urns, and other assorted brassware. These they borrowed from anyone who had them, irrespective of their suku. In most cases these items would be loaned without charge even when borrowed from other than a Piliang. The cushions and carpets were to cover the floor of a portion of the ancestral house (one of the few to survive the fire) where the ceremony would be staged. This portion would be completely separated from the rest of the house by curtains and canopy which, as the collective property of the community, could be borrowed without charge.

Datuak Maleko further estimated to me and interested bystanders that some three hundred large plates, five hundred small plates, and five hundred glasses had to be rented. These would be rented for a moderate fee either from a small private enterprise or from a local religious organization. More difficult to obtain, but crucially important, were the large decorated platters from which the panghulu would eat.

Various sorts of musical instruments were essential—in particular, a large gong to hang in front of the ancestral house. This gong is sounded only at the ascension of a panghulu and gives notice, not only within the community but to neighboring villages, of what is transpiring.

While Datuak Maleko and the Four Women assembled these, Firdaus's mother, Nasma, and several of the women of her periuak were beginning to buy nonperishable foods such as coconuts, spices, peppers, and onions, and to make arrangements soon to buy meat, fish, and other perishables. Datuak Maleko gave estimates to me and the rest of his audience on my porch of just what prodigious quantities of food were required for a fete of this size: 80 kilos (later, in fact, increased to 100) of beef, 200 kilos of fish, 30 kilos of peppers, 30 kilos of onions, 500 coconuts, 5 kilos of ginger, and so on. Although before the baralek panghulu was over, Datuak Maleko had found his responsibilities somewhat burdensome, at this point he was obviously enjoying both his strategic importance and the opportunity to describe to me and others the nature and especially, the magnitude of the preparations.

Thursday, March 6

Perhaps the most conspicuous project on this Thursday was the construction of a ceremonial arch outside Firdaus's ancestral house. In this work, some thirty men participated. Virtually everyone emphasized to me that this work was *gotong royong*, an example of mutual help by the community at large, and as proof pointed to all those present who were not from the Piliang suku. However, it should be noted that few, if any, individuals came or were regarded as coming simply because they were members of the community. All had particular ties to the sponsors. Those ties, though, did not compel or obligate attendance since, for instance, of the seventeen to twenty urang sumando who attended the Piliang large meeting (and still more had been invited), only eight helped erect the ceremonial arch; likewise, many more men attended the meeting of the group of Firdaus's father than worked on the ceremonial arch. The hosts, of course, hoped that attendance would be large, both as demonstration of their good standing in the community and as a supply of labor, but they certainly did not expect everyone invited to attend. The most the hosts could do was to cast their net widely so that no one felt snubbed.

The ceremonial arch went up quickly, the men working with reasonable diligence and apparent enjoyment. Panghulu, too, pitched in, as is indeed appropriate at gotong royong, but in such a way that they still preserved their dignity. They gave advice and direction, helped to steady a support, and such. They did not, however, engage in really heavy or dirty work. Firdaus observed on the periphery, often acting as dignified host in attendance at a table with its welcoming decorated cloth and brass urn filled with betel and cigarettes. When I inquired of a bystander why Firdaus himself was not helping to construct the arch, I was told that his anak buah would be ashamed for him to do so. Many of the themes of the ambalau and baralek panghulu concern treating the panghulu like a raja, since he is said to be like a raja—or, in an effort to be more contemporary, a president—to his anak buah. In these preparations for his ceremony of ascension, Firdaus was learning and being helped to learn how to enact the basic relationship of panghulu to anak bush: the panghulu provides control, the anak buah, energy.

The ceremonial arch is raised by members of the community.

At 10:30, after about an hour-and-a-half of work, we were all called inside the ancestral house for the collective meal that must follow any privately solicited gotong royong. All the men ate together food purchased by the hosts and cooked by the women of Firdaus's periuak. Some ate only a little, but all ate, including a few who seemed to have come just for the meal. No one would ever be excluded from such a meal. One apparently harmless impoverished mad man never seemed to miss one of these free meals, although he did not in any way participate in the preceding activities. Gotong royong and commensality would seem to imply each other, and are the clearest ways that the community is defined. After all, a basic form of baso basi (which if omitted breaks one's connection with the community) is to proffer commensality by offering to share food and drink with all those present.

While the men had been working on the ceremonial arch and eating, women, too, had engaged in gotong royong both inside and outside the house, grinding spices, scraping ginger, peeling garlic. I had thought that the men rather enjoyed their collective work on

The collective labor of women includes grinding spices to feed ascension guests.

the arch, but the women were really having fun, either playing very catchy rhythms on small gongs, tambourines, or a pop bottle with a spoon jiggled in its neck, or in following the rhythms with their heavy stone pestles.

The ceremonial enclosure for the seclusion of the panghulu is erected.

Friday, March 7

By mid-afternoon both men and women were erecting within the ancestral house the *tabia*, the ceremonial enclosure of canopy and curtains which provides seclusion for the panghulu. The ceremonial enclosure is the ritual fixture of central importance at both the ambalau and baralek panghulu. The six strips composing the canopy refer, according to one, to the six suku in Bayur. Canopy and curtains are draped over and loosely stitched to a light bamboo frame, in such a way that one of the house pillars is enclosed within the somewhat flimsy walls. Again according to this same informant, adaik requires that one pillar be so enclosed. This pillar is like the baringin tree (banyan tree), an often-cited image of the panghulu. (The panghulu provides shelter and support for his anak buah, as does the spreading baringin tree in the midst of the plain.) Not surprisingly, others on whom I tried this interpretation disagreed: the pillar, one said, was just to hold up the roof; another said that no pillars would be even better than one, as the view would be less obstructed.

However, agreement was remarkably broad about what the ceremonial enclosure meant. Everyone I talked to—both men and women—said that it must have no rips or tears (some of which were undergoing repair as the enclosure was erected) because it was to keep out the air. This image was generally understood to mean that no outside influence could be allowed to affect the deliberations of the panghulu within, and hence the course of adaik.

The final touch outside the house was to hang six red, white, and black streamers—the Minang colors, I was told—by the ceremonial arch. Several men later said that the six streamers refer to the six suku; others said that six were all they had been able to borrow from a neighboring town.

The fact that at least some suggested that the six streamers referred to the six suku of Bayur can be regarded as illustrating the more general theme that the entire community considered itself to be taking some degree of responsibility for this most quintessentially adaik ceremony. Responsibility was, of course, most heavily vested with Firdaus and his periuak, but it did extend to encompass the entire town of Bayur, and even in the most pervasive sense, as shown by the willingness of a neighboring village to cooperate, the community composed of all Minangkabau. It is after all, adaik that makes community life itself possible, and adaik which makes it reasonable for Minang anywhere to live as Minang.

THE CEREMONY OF ASCENSION: THE SOLIDIFICATION OF SOCIAL FORM

In the ambalau and the baralek panghulu an even greater emphasis is placed on acting according to social form. At this time, virtually all activities of the protagonists are regarded as determined by adaik. Both spectators and protagonists alike regard the pervasively formal conduct of the protagonists as the most truly Minang of Minang behavior.

Saturday, March 8

The formality was apparent immediately after the arrival of Firdaus just before 9:00 A.M. in front of his ancestral house. He sat motionless outside in the full panghulu regalia of turban, sash, *kris* (dagger), and embroidered pants and shirt. A few minutes later, six panghulu arrived at the ceremonial arch. At that point a brass urn was presented by one of the Four Men and each was asked to help himself to the contents. These panghulu also were in full regalia and obviously had planned to arrive together at the appropriate moment: I had seen them earlier, waiting in a coffee shop down the road. They were escorted under the arch and given seats next to Firdaus. Soon they were joined by five more panghulu, and all twelve began to engage in quiet, rather stiff conversation. Their composure was all the more impressive because of the context: the ancestral house, including its windows, was packed with excitedly conversing women; the front yard—at a respectful distance from the panghulu, to be sure—had by now filled with men, women, boys and girls, all milling about. Datuak Maleko, assistant panghulu and hence ineligible to enter the ceremonial enclosure, did not sit with the other panghulu in apparent tranquility; instead he bustled around, harried, still active in his role of principal organizer and coordinator for the Piliang hosts. Soon he arranged for Jhon to take a picture of all the panghulu, posed in a line, with Firdaus in the center.

After the photograph had been taken, the panghulu ascended the righthand and more prestigious of the two outside staircases of the ancestral house. The orator, carrying a brass urn, escorted each to his place inside the ceremonial enclosure. He seated the guest panghulu first, beginning with their representative, Datuak Mudo, who as chairman of the Bayur panghulu was given the seat of honor at the center of the back of the enclosure. Datuak Batuah followed. As assistant chairman he received the seat at the left side of his principal. The most senior of the guest panghulu, Datuak Sati, was given a place of honor on Datuak Mudo's right, still along the back wall; he was followed by the other guest panghulu, who completed the seating on the back and side walls. Last to be seated were the host Piliang panghulu, with Firdaus, the prospective Datuak Bandaro, and then his assistant and successor Samsul Bahri, the prospective Datuak Marahun, bringing up the rear.

The orator who directed this seating was Sutan Jahaidin, perhaps the best known of the three or four men in Bayur who were regarded as expert in ceremonial—indirect—speech. He had been hired by the hosts to represent them and to act as master of ceremonies.

As soon as everyone was seated, the orator began by welcoming the now secluded guests. For the next half hour the panghulu talked among themselves about whether they could smoke and about whether they should raise the curtains of the enclosure so that fresh air could come in from the windows along the front of the house. All Minang adult males are heavy smokers, and it was a foregone conclusion that the panghulu would agree to allow smoking. In fact, when they entered, by each seat was an unopened pack of cigarettes. Similarly, no panghulu could long survive in his thick regalia inside an entirely sealed enclosure. Nevertheless, both matters were subject to deliberation. Men, women, and children, largely but not exclusively of the hosts, crowded around the sides of the enclosure, peeking through a few unrepaired rips, straining to see and hear. But even the panghulu were having some difficulty hearing each other, having often to lean forward in their seats toward the speaker. Although some, like Datuak Maleko, circulated among the unseen audience shushing conversations, whispering and the sounds of continuing work (such as the apparently unending task of grinding spices) created considerable background noise. The panghulu, however, continued to talk in ordinary tones, although not in ordinary language, not acknowledging the proximity and noise of those on the other side of the enclosure.

After about a half-hour devoted to the welcome and the deliberation concerning smoking and ventilation, consensus was reached, and the Four Men lifted the enclosure curtain, not only on the side adjacent to the windows but on the side facing the interior of the house. The interior of the enclosure, with the panghulu now discreetly puffing on their cigarettes, was open to the community. Their appearance was hardly relaxed, however, as they continued to sit, virtually motionless, cross-legged, with their knees parallel with their sitting mats.

The following excerpts from the much longer tape I made of the proceedings should convey a sense of the extreme formality of ceremonial speech. There is extensive use of set phrases and established metaphors to convey information already known by all; there is respect and deference for the others present, expressed in elaborate but standard images; and there is the actual description of the role of panghulu, conveyed in major part through allusions. These statements show the Minang of Bayur at their most oblique and refined, on this their most adaik of occasions.

These excerpts, taken in order, begin with the first question to be decided after the side of the enclosure was raised: should Jhon and I be allowed to enter, he to take photographs and I to tape-record and observe close at hand.

> *Sutan Jahaidin:* We request that the photographer and Fred enter the ceremonial enclosure so that the photographer is free to stand and to sit.
>
> *Datuak Mudo:* It is respectfully submitted to Datuak Sati, Datuak Tumanggung, and all the panghulu inside the enclosure and all the hosts who are inside the house. Formerly there was no photography here [in Bayur] but now there is. This is a new procedure and we must first reach consensus about it. [Very brief pause while Datuak Mudo reached a consensus with the men sitting next to him.] And now we give permission for the photographer and Fred to enter the enclosure. It is respectfully submitted to Sutan Jahaidin. That which is round, rolls, while that which is flat, glides. [Just as objects follow their nature, so too should humans. In this case, humans should fulfill their capacity to reach consensus before acting.] Because a photographer does not contradict adaik or religion we give permission for him to take photographs.
>
> *Datuak Mudo:* Respectful greetings to Datuak Majo Lelo, Datuak Pamuncak, Imam Chatib, and all of the hosts in this ancestral house and Sutan Jahaidin. The round is rolled, the flat is glided. Sutan Jahaidin, in the name of the hosts, has responded. Delicious betel nut is eaten; pleasing talk is expressed. This talk that is expressed is true. We must follow that which is proper and fitting, that which follows the path of adaik. If we do not follow this, then the bird's nest will not be built low. [This refers to a variety of bird which builds its nest low to the ground to gain the protection of earth-dwelling wasps; thus, just as this bird has a reason for building its nest in this way, so too do those present have a reason for having this ambalau.] It will be pleasing to the heart to do, and pleasing to the eye to see if we make a work that is good, one we do together.
>
> *Sutan Jahaidin:* Respectful greetings to Datuak Alat Cumano, Datuak Sati, Datuak Mudo, Datuak Batuah, Datuak Rajo Malintang,

Datuak Majo Lelo, esteemed Imam Bagindo [a sampling of those present], who all sit in a square, sit on the floor, in the places I requested. Genuine respect comes from me. It is not the case that I pass quickly by the elders, but my work is to give the response of the hosts. I am connected to the tongue of the hosts in order to advance the splendid work here. Therefore, those here now, those most surely invited, those who come later, those already arrived give great, immeasurable pleasure to us. Our intention in inviting the panghulu to come here is for the implementation of our fine plan. For this we are all here. The previous Datuak Bandaro has already died, and been changed again and again, until now it has descended to our matrikin Firdaus who will become Datuak Bandaro. Because the day is already advanced and the time for prayer almost arrived, now we exclude the tip, now we exclude the base, and only take all that is essential. Formerly, the one who became Datuak Bandaro was Mokmin, who was replaced by Munir [the previous titleholder], and now Munir surrenders Datuak Bandaro to Firdaus. A shoot will grow even if broken off; ancestral inheritance also descends [a proverb]. In this way also, the ancestral title of Datuak Bandaro descends to our matrikin who is named Firdaus. Munir thus gave it to Firdaus because he was abroad. And now the one named Firdaus we will install as Datuak Bandaro and Samsul Bahri we install as Datuak Marahun.

Datuak Mudo: The ancient histories from grandparent to mother's brother, from mother's brother descended to sister's child, the inheritance which we receive as guardians from the elders. The world of the Minangkabau circles Mount Marapi, is wrapped by Batang Bangkaweh [name of a river], is passed by the sound of waves breaking, here the durian tree was slashed by the raja [who made boundaries by cutting down trees], here is the honey bee at Aia Bangih [name of a town]. Crossed pieces of wood in the middle of the cooking fire; there the fire lives [truth comes through discussion, from the exchange of views]. Long with short talk we have combined so that we can take all that is needed. I will not talk at length; everything I have to say has been said. I hope that Datuak Bandaro has taken what he needs from what I have said. I hope that Datuak Bandaro will use it and a drop becomes an ocean, a handful of sand becomes a mountain. That is all from me.

Datuak Sati [the most senior of the guest panghulu]: And I speak here in the name of the forty-four panghulu of the village of Bayur,

the Imam Chatib, the intellectuals, and all the inhabitants of the
village of Bayur of that which I can clarify for all of you today; you
today have already been elevated to become Datuak Bandaro at the
spot where your anak buah will report to you about adaik matters
[this present ancestral house]. All of you sit equally low, all of you
stand equally high with all the panghulu in the community of Bayur.
If sick, sick together; if happy, happy together; if insulted, insulted
together with the other forty-three panghulu. You have been elevated
to become a panghulu, not just from suku Piliang alone. You must
also join in the projects of other suku, not just in the village of
Bayur, but generally throughout the Minang world. The boundaries
of the sea where waves break, up to the durian tree slashed by the
raja at Aia Bangih—there you will be a panghulu [a panghulu
throughout all of the Minangkabau world]. As a panghulu you should
not be seen only by your anak buah; also by other suku you should
be seen. If your anak buah do wrong, fix the blame; if right, fix the
credit. You are like the baringin tree in the middle of the plain, the
leaves of which shade from the heat and protect from the rain; the
trunk is a place to lean. Your wife must be clever and give advice
to you who are becoming panghulu. If you are not true in carrying
out adaik, you will be struck by the oath and the poison of the kris,
the emblem of the greatness of Minangkabau panghulu, possessed
by Datuak Perpatih nan Sabatang and Datuak Ketemanggungan [the
two primevil panghulu]. If you are not true to adaik, [you will be as
a tree and] on the top, buds will not sprout; on the bottom, sap will
not circulate; in the middle, bumblebees will bore holes. [This sen-
tence constitutes the oath of office.] Thus will strike the poison
descended from Datuak Perpatih nan Sabatang and Datuak Ketemanggungan. I hope that you accept all of my advice, that a drop
becomes an ocean, a handful of sand becomes a mountain.

Datuak Bandaro: Respectful greeting to Datuak Sati, Datuak Mudo,
Datuak Batuah, Datuak Rajo Malintang, Datuak Majo Lelo, and
other persons inside this ceremonial enclosure. All the advice which
has been given to me because I have ascended to become Datuak
Bandaro I will accept; I will carry out the obligation which there is
for me with my full energy and thought; and I accept the poison
oath. I will carry out in the capacity of panghulu everything that
becomes my obligation to my anak buah and to the village. I say
many thanks to the panghulu who have given advice and I will carry
it out well. A drop becomes an ocean, a handful of sand becomes

a mountain. At night I will take it to my pillow; during the day I will take it along with my cane. And I ask Allah that I will not be in error; that adaik will be carried out by me as Datuak Bandaro. And may I not do anything that is in opposition to adaik. Peace be with you.

The most elaborate images and archaic Minang words came at the beginning of the ambalau. Certainly this was the portion of my tape which Jhon had greatest difficulty understanding; it was, in fact, necessary for us to consult several individuals in order to piece together any meaning. The most elaborate and, I think, esoteric image in the portion I recorded was of the purposeful bird that builds its nest near the ground-dwelling wasps. Many of the proverbs, however, are very well known: that which is round, rolls, while that which is flat, glides; the drop becomes an ocean, the handful of sand becomes a mountain. These are commonly heard on ceremonial occasions, as is the response of taking advice to one's pillow at night and with one's cane during the day. The voluminosity of adaik (and, by implication, of one's knowledge of adaik) is often mentioned in both ceremonial and nonceremonial contexts. The panghulu in the enclosure said that they were only presenting the central aspects of adaik on this occasion, since time was limited; Datuak Rajo Panghulu, in his talk in Bayur, similarly said that he could talk indefinitely about adaik, but this time would give only the essence.

Minang often refer in their speeches to aspects of their history by mentioning some of the locations which mark their traditional boundaries. The concern with showing unbroken continuity with the past is particularly apparent at the ascension of a panghulu, an occasion regarded as undiluted adaik: the ceremony of ascension is regarded as a precise replication of original practice. A narrower demonstration of continuity came with the identification of the previous, current, and future holders of the title Datuak Bandaro. Moreover, the concern so frequently expressed (although not in any of these excerpts) by the Bayur panghulu that their number be at its full strength of forty-four not only suggests the continuing importance of the panghulu in the Minang conception of social order, but also, I think, indicates yet again the importance of maintaining continuity with past practice and hence of remaining within adaik.

The oath of office in which the new panghulu was compared to a tree, was delivered to Firdaus by Datuak Sati, the most senior of those guest panghulu present. Every indication I have, including the solemnity with which Firdaus himself responded to the oath, suggests that the image of a tree—or a life—overwhelmed with affliction and misfortune is one compelling serious thought about the importance of the panghulu's responsibility to carry out adaik.

The panghulu conveyed as much elegance and indirection of expression in their speech as they were capable of. One of the reasons that Datuak Mudo and Datuak Batuah were selected chairman and vice-chairman of the Bayur panghulu was because they are among the best of the local orators. However, in what was, I think, an accurate and by no means hostile appraisal, none of these men was regarded as truly expert. None, including Sutan Jahaidin, who was in a very minor way a professional, could keep up for very long the stream of proverb and verse which should characterize adaik speaking. Other limitations were recognized by some listeners, who said that much of their Minang was insufficiently archaic, their speeches being liberally laced with Indonesian and words that are both Indonesian and Minang. Granted that their phrasing might have been more elaborate and less contemporary, their conversation was nevertheless a clear departure from everyday speech. With the exception of the oath, very little in particular needed to be said, since what little was actually communicated was already known by everyone. Certainly the current identities of Datuak Bandaro and Datuak Marahun (a subject which in fact appears with great frequency in the full transcript of the speeches) were hardly in doubt.

The fact that form took such precedence over content in speech had its parallel in so exaggerated an emphasis on the other forms of baso basi as to constitute a clear departure from everyday life. The pattern of giving respectful greetings to a representative sample of those present, of apologizing when speaking for possibly cutting someone else off, of seeking consensus for every decision no matter how trivial, all constitute a kind of quintessential baso basi as a necessary component of a ceremony of quintessential adaik.

Following these speeches came a long prayer in Arabic, and then Sutan Jahaidin inquired whether the guests would like to eat. Then, when Datuak Mudo announced that the guests had agreed through consensus that they wished to do so, the Four Men cleared space to make way for the food. (One Minang talking with me about the importance of consensus mentioned with some amusement that Minang find consensus necessary to reach a conclusion even as foregone as wishing to eat.) These four proceeded to bring in brass pitchers and bowls to be used for hand washing after the meal and then the food itself, covered, on high brass trays called *dulang*. They placed the first dulang in front of Datuak Mudo and then, on his right, a covered platter containing additional food.

When serving was completed, the curtain of the enclosure was lowered so that the panghulu would not be seen by their anak buah, the ordinary people. "They are eating in the way of a raja," I was told. "It would not be correct and orderly to do otherwise." Furthermore, the meal once concluded, the leftovers were covered, so that when the Four Men conveyed them back to the Four Women no one could see how much or how little the panghulu had actually eaten. The Four Women threw all the leftovers into the garbage: no one else should see or consume them. Thus, the purely organic quality of the panghulu was suppressed in this most formal context.

The formality of this convocation of panghulu also appeared in their table manners. Not only was a panghulu expected to observe the restraint of ordinary baso basi by letting the food touch only his fingertips and not his palm, but, on this occasion, as his right hand approached his lips, he was also to toss rather than place his food into his mouth. In this way no saliva touched his hand, which might then be conveyed back into the food from which others were eating. That several men ate together from a single dulang and platter meant, I was told later, that there is only one adaik. Another, although compatible, significance might be that the same kind of unity of panghulu created by the seclusion within the enclosure and the extreme emphasis on consensus is both depicted and created by an extreme emphasis on commensality.

As with all other Minang ceremonies I saw, the meal concluded the business at hand. After a short bit of leave-taking between the orator and Datuak Mudo, the panghulu rose. Datuak Bandaro, and

Within the ceremonial enclosure dining is at its most refined.

then Datuak Marahun, shook hands with each of the panghulu as they filed out of the ceremonial enclosure. Once outside, the pang-hulu were again posed for a commemorative photograph.

Despite flowery speeches earlier (not included in the excerpts) suggesting that this ambalau would last all night, the session had adjourned by about 2:00 P.M. Nonetheless, those in the ceremonial enclosure had stiffly sweltered for almost four hours. I talked later that day with Datuak Batuah, who proudly stressed the hardships the panghulu had endured to carry through the ceremony as pre-scribed by adaik. He referred to the heat and, in particular, to the pain of sitting with knees flat for such a long period of time. To judge by my own aching numbness and the expression of sup-pressed pain on the faces of the others, expecially the older pang-hulu, the seclusion had indeed been a physical trial. When I inquired of Datuak Batuah why fewer panghulu had attended than I had been led to expect, I was told that many had simply chosen to avoid such an ordeal. Datuak Batuah also emphasized to me

how oblique—how filled with archaic language and hidden allusions—the speeches had been—so oblique that only a Minangkabau and no other Indonesian would have been able to understand
them at all. This conversation suggested that a clear link existed
for him between acceptance of constraint, obliqueness, and distinctive Minang identity.

Although hosts focused their attention, energy, and resources
on providing faultlessly for those in the ceremonial enclosure, they
also had to meet other major responsibilities. After those in the
enclosure began eating, it was permissible, and in fact necessary,
to serve food to the scores of other people in the house.

If there had been only the ambalau and not a baralek panghulu
as well, the ambalau would have concluded with Firdaus, now a
fully accredited panghulu, walking a circuit through the streets of
Bayur in the company of the other panghulu and Datuak Marahun.
As it was, this public presentation of the new Datuak Bandaro was
reserved until the baralek panghulu the next day.

The final event of this day of the ambalau anticipated the baralek
panghulu. Specific to the baralek is a three-tiered construction of
siriah leaves (one of the essential ingredients of the betel nut
mixture) called *siriah gadang*. A Piliang woman, one of the few
women in Bayur with the requisite skill, had for days been stitching
together the intricate arrangement of leaves. Just before 5:00 P.M.,
a procession of women, led by three women striking small gongs
in complex unison, carried the completed siriah gadang along the
main street of Bayur to the ancestral house, where it remained
until the baralek panghulu.

This procession of women was a prelude to a simply enormous
parade of women the following day, especially younger women
dressed in a kind of traditional finery called *bapolot*. Since this
finery was usually inherited, that late afternoon was a time for the
minor alterations often necessary to fit the garment to someone of
the new generation. Certainly in my landlady's house, and I was
told throughout town, such preparations were greeted with excitement, as ever greater numbers of the community prepared to participate in the ascension of Datuak Bandaro.

Sunday, March 9

The baralek panghulu began in much the same way as had the
ambalau. Shortly after 9:00 A.M., Datuak Bandaro arrived in full
regalia at his ancestral house. This time, however, he was in the

company of a less spectacularly dressed Datuak Marahun. Each shook hands with the host panghulu, who were already present. I heard Datuak Tamajo Basa, an important Piliang panghulu, tell Datuak Bandaro to be sure to shake the hands of the panghulu as they arrived. Datuak Bandaro nodded in assent to this reminder of elementary baso basi. Datuak Tamajo Basa then continued his preceremonial fussing by having Datuak Bandaro exchange with Datuak Pamuncak, a Piliang panghulu, for a bigger and better kris. Datuak Maleko, still the Piliang program coordinator, paced about making periodic excursions to the ceremonial arch to see who might be coming up the road. I sensed a concern, even greater than for the ambalau, that everything be just right. After all, the baralek panghulu is put on entirely for show.

A few minutes later, the guest panghulu arrived together, arranging themselves in two rows outside the arch. One of the Four Men appeared immediately to present the brass urn and decorated cloth first to Datuak Mudo standing in the middle of the first row, then to the panghulu on his right, and then to the rest. As these visitors passed through the arch and approached the table, Datuak Bandaro and Datuak Marahun rose and shook their hands. Promptly thereafter a soldier, standing at the foot of the righthand staircase, fired three shots into the air to encourage any tardy panghulu to make haste, because once the panghulu are sequestered within the ceremonial enclosure no one ordinarily is allowed to enter.

After a grace period of perhaps five minutes, Datuak Bandaro, followed by Datuak Marahun, moved to the righthand side of the right staircase; opposite them on the lefthand side of this same staircase stood one of the Four Men holding a brass urn with decorated cloth. The guest panghulu, followed by the host panghulu, filed up the staircase past the rather stiffly smiling Datuak Bandaro and Datuak Marahun. At the landing inside the house, they were escorted with the brass urn to their seats inside the enclosure in essentially the order of precedence in which they had already arranged themselves. By 10:30, when the last were seated, the enclosure curtain fell back into place, sealing them off. The proceedings within the enclosure and the rest of the ancestral house were much the same as during the ambalau. What few differences there were emphasized that the purpose of the baralek panghulu

Panghulu pose for a group portrait after the ceremony of ascension.

was to announce to the community at large that there was a new panghulu. For instance, although the community was still physically excluded from the ceremonial enclosure, this time an additional orator was sequestered within to act as their spokesman. As with the ambalau, the early discussion within the enclosure concerned whether the panghulu might smoke and open the enclosure to air and to view. Again, the house was packed with men and women crowding around and peeking through the small rips in the curtain. The same formal speaking was followed by the same secluded formal dining of the panghulu and the same general feeding of those outside the ceremonial enclosure. The conclusion of this most formal stage of the ceremony was again marked by a group portrait of all the panghulu posed in front of the ceremonial arch.

However, what followed the emergence of the panghulu from the enclosure and from their portrait was dramatically different this time. To the thundering of the gong accompanied by a drum band, the panghulu set out to tour Bayur, led by the Piliang panghulu, with Datuak Bandaro in the center of the first row and Datuak Marahun on his left. This was to "introduce Datuak Bandaro to the town of Bayur."

Datuak Bandaro, Datuak Marahun, and their colleagues led an immense throng of men, women, and children. Some had left the ancestral house with them, but many joined from the crowds which had collected outside the houses and shops. The parade looped through town and returned along the main road to the ancestral house, escorted home by the sounding of a big gong. Datuak Bandaro and Datuak Marahun then seated themselves in two of the chairs outside the house to await the parade from the bako—the Guci suku of Firdaus's father.

As the bako parade began, a small boy of about seven, named Andoko, was lifted up onto the horse. He had been selected for an eminence he did not seem greatly to cherish simply because he was a small, manageable boy from the periuak of Firdaus's father. Virtually everyone with whom I talked about this parade emphasized the central importance of the boy on horseback. Most explained both the horse and the boy's attire, particularly his golden crown, as suggesting the accoutrements of a raja. That panghulu were like raja, and that this boy had some connection with Firdaus Datuak Bandaro, was generally recognized. But I had great difficulty in finding anyone who could say specifically what this connection was, to account for the boy himself being dressed and conveyed like a diminutive raja. An answer, when it finally came from Sutan Zara Endah, was primarily directed to several other features of the bako parade for which I had also not been able to receive an explanation: I had, for example, wanted to know why the siriah gadang was carried in the parade, and, moreover, carried not just by any woman, as some said, but by a woman married to a member of the bako—the father's kin group. He said it is carried in the bako parade because the siriah gadang "as a source of honor exceeding the siriah within the brass urn indicates the greatness of the panghulu. Siriah gadang makes things orderly." It is carried by a woman because: "Women have children; the bako are joyous because one of their children has become a panghulu." Sutan Zara Endah then went on to explain that the boy is the child of the bako, just as is Firdaus, the new panghulu.

However, in view of this interpretation one might expect the parallel between Firdaus and Andoko to be somewhat tighter: Andoko should be the child of a woman married into the bako—

as was Firdaus—rather than the child of a woman herself of the bako—for the same reason that the siriah gadang is carried by such a woman. Such a tidiness of pattern was clearly not necessary to the participants. For them, the realization that this parade commemorated both Firdaus Datuak Bandaro and his father's family was sufficient.

This parade was even larger than the preceding one for Datuak Bandaro, since the bako were joined by hundreds of women dressed in the traditional finery of bapolot.

An uneasy-looking Andoko, steadied on only a saddle blanket by several men, while the owner led his horse, headed the parade. The foremost in the cluster of men following were the bako panghulu of the Guci suku, still in their regalia.

The women, led by the one selected to carry the siriah gadang, followed. This parade, too, circled through the town so that all could see, and even greater numbers attached themselves to the procession. Many of the men in the lead group were whooping; the all-percussion band was thumping its loudest; on all sides, hundreds, perhaps thousands, of shouting men, women, and children followed the procession as best they could through the narrow streets. As we approached the ancestral house of the new Datuak Bandaro, the drums and gongs continued to boom. Then the visitors were met with a brass urn; the siriah gadang was carried into the house, followed by all of the women up the left staircase. The men, along with Andoko, entered the house by the right staircase and took seats around the siriah gadang on the cushions underneath the now-raised side-curtains of the ceremonial enclosure.

The volume of those inside the house was so great that several of the men still outside dashed underneath to check the recently installed supports. Of the males, Andoko was the first to be served, presumably as a surrogate panghulu, the guest of central importance in the bako parade. Then the other panghulu all ate from the high brass trays. The other men and all of the women also ate, but from ordinary plates. Again, all the food was provided by the Piliang. Some formal speaking among the men followed the meal, but it was too noisy for anyone, including the responding speakers, to have much idea of what was said. By 5:00 P.M. most started home, the baralek panghulu concluding in fine style.

A throng of women parade to celebrate the ascension of Firdaus.

As I left, I asked Datuak Maleko how he was; he said he was tired, had a headache, and was calling it a day. I managed to get home just before a heavy rain started, and from the shelter of my porch a few minutes later saw the last of the departing guests. Most were running. But not the panghulu. They maintained a measured pace, conscious of their dignity even throughout a downpour.

The ritual of ascension is, above all, a formal and ordered transition. The new panghulu is selected from the periuak whose turn has come in the pattern of rotation; the ritual and its preliminaries present the anak buah at their most dutiful and the panghulu at their most composed. The various kinship groups, both within the host and the guest suku, act and are treated in different ways, largely according to their degree of genealogical proximity to the ascending panghulu. These distinctions, however, are also juxtaposed with frequent reference to the community at large. That Bayur is composed of a single community is recognized by the emphasis placed on communal cooperation of gotong royong, by the inclusion of an orator for the community within the ceremonial enclosure during the baralek panghulu, and by the parade through the village, which has the explicit intent of introducing the new panghulu to the community and is not only watched but joined by anyone from the community who wishes.

The ritual enacts social form, and by so doing, demonstrates to the new panghulu and others that the panghulu is to reflect and create order. In addition, it suggests the intellectual basis of that order. During their speeches, the panghulu and orators display, in concentrated form, a way of thinking about the world, a way of making interpretations. These interpretations sometimes consist largely of the aphorisms and verses which are often presented as simply true and, at other times—as in the discussion of whether the photographer should be admitted—as interpretations of particular cimcumstances. Throughout, truth is continually recreated, not only by the enactment of and reference to quintessential—condensed—adaik, but by the most scrupulous observance of the social and intellectual principle of consensus.

The panghulu ascension ceremony provides the most definitive Minangkabau statement—and demonstration—of what, at its most formal and ordered, their society is. This ceremony, along with the pig hunt indicates the maximum contrast between order and disorder, constraint and energy, possible in Minangkabau society.

Chapter 7
The Pig Hunt: Energy, Form, and Order

Pig hunting is regarded by the Minangkabau as a quintessentially male activity. Males of any age are welcome: boys often accompany their fathers; very old men participate if they are still vigorous. Bayur, along with most if not all Minang villages, has a hunt association with a chairman elected by the local hunters. Also, as is typical, the Bayur group belongs to a larger association of neighboring villages, each of which periodically acts as host to the other member villages. News of the local weekly hunt is circulated by mail to each village-hunt chairman, who then informs the membership.

The hunt headquarters in Bayur is in a coffee shop. Here the location and time of the next hunt are posted each week, and here is stored the association flag, a blue banner with white letters bought by the local hunters, which in translation reads "Bayur Pig-Hunting Association." The most avid of the hunters tend to frequent this coffee shop, and the chairman can be found there almost every evening.

The hunt I attended was a special invitational hunt, not in the local sequence: it was part of a community project to raise money for the construction of a school and police station. The hunt publicized the project, bringing outsiders into the area so that they might patronize a fund-raising fair and possibly donate building materials. The Bayur contingent, for instance, contributed several pieces of roofing metal. The hunters anticipated superlative pig hunting, because this hunt was to take place some thirty-five miles from Bayur in an especially wild area known for its abundance of pigs.

Early in the morning on the appointed Sunday, about twenty-

Pig hunting is regarded as a quintessentially male activity.

five men, each with at least one dog, gathered in front of the hunt coffee shop. (Although the attendance was somewhat better than usual, it was still only a small fraction of Bayur's male population of many hundred.) The dogs were barking, straining at their leashes, and snapping at each other. The men were of all ages, and wore rough clothing and often strips of cloth or turbans on their heads to keep sweat and hair out of their eyes. All were armed, most with hunting knives in belt sheaths, some with spears or hand axes. (A very few men have old rifles, so sometimes firearms are carried on a hunt.)

We left Bayur in one of the local buses chartered for the occasion. Once we were underway, the dogs settled down, but the men maintained a high pitch of excitement and enthusiasm, emitting frequent and raucous whoops, particularly whenever the bus passed through a village. The association flag had been strapped to the bus, proclaiming the identity of the passengers; the driver played tunes almost continually on the battery of air horns with which the bus was equipped. (I was told by the hunt chairman that a special point is always made to charter a bus with an outstanding set of horns, as these contribute to the festivity of the trip.) Even during the bus trip I was much struck by the rowdiness of the group. The men acted rather like a marauding horde sweeping through the countryside. Informants did, in fact, characterize this conduct on the bus and the general tone of the pig hunt as crude, unrefined, and unconstrained. Certainly there are Minang who do customarily act this way—parewa in particular—but this is the only public occasion that I know of in which such crude conduct sets the dominant tone, even for those men who normally pride themselves on their refinement and constraint. For instance, there were on the bus several schoolteachers and panghulu, including my host, the hunt chairman. (They were specifically pointed out to me as such by the chairman.) All of these men were also dressed in rough clothing and acted no more decorously than the others. The hunt is democratic: men are not excluded or discriminated against on the grounds of wealth, refinement, age, title, or kinship group. All are welcome, and all behave with the good-natured crudity that habitually characterizes only a few members of the community. Since Minang are adept at altering their behavior to fit the context, I doubt that any of the participants on the pig hunt felt strain at the relaxation of standards of conduct.

Yet even on the pig hunt this crudity is interspersed by reversion to very refined ceremonial etiquette and oratory. When we arrived at our destination, we were welcomed as distinguished visitors by our hosts—the home pig-hunting association—and were offered refreshment and highly deferential speeches of welcome, to which the spokesman of each of the several guest groups responded with an appreciative formal reply. (The spokesman of each group is simply someone expert in formal speech who comes forward on this particular occasion. Sutan Jahaidin, an avid pig hunter, spoke for Bayur.) But once this formal exchange was over—and it lasted only about twenty minutes—the hunt began and rough-and-ready conduct was resumed.

Each village pig-hunting association has, in addition to the chairman who organizes the meets, charters the bus, and so on, a man in charge of the hunt itself, a *muncak rajo*. During a hunt, all of the hunt leaders of the visiting groups move through the woods in the company of, but slightly subordinate to, the hunt leader of the host group. These men and their dogs do the active foraging for pigs, and when a pig is flushed or a fresh trail found, the host hunt leader shouts out to the main body of waiting hunters to release their dogs. The dogs are in a frenzy by this time, because the excited sounds of those few men and dogs in hot pursuit can be clearly heard. When let go, they dash off at full speed, closely followed by their almost equally excited masters. On the hunt that I witnessed, the first time the dogs were released, a very frightened calf, followed by its distressed mother, emerged from a thicket, surrounded by yapping, snarling dogs. Neither cow nor calf was injured, although the hunters, who seemed to be enjoying the frenzy and ferocity of the attack, did not immediately call off their dogs. A few farmers several hundred yards away in an isolated rice paddy neither did nor could have done anything to intervene. One of the local hunters shouted to them the distinctly partial truth that it was the Bayur hunters who had been thus mistreating their animals.

This hunt was not as successful as hoped, and it was not until late in the day that a pig was killed. The group of hunters from Bayur that I was with had temporarily dropped out of the main group for some refreshment at a small coffee shop on the edge of one of the villages we had passed. But hearing a great racket of dogs and men, we rushed to a large bamboo thicket in a grazing area only a few hundred yards from the village. All of the dogs and a few of the men were darting in and out of the thicket. I was excitedly told that lots of dogs were being wounded—a measure of the formidability of the pig and the courage of the dogs. I was also warned that I should be prepared to run and climb a tree if the pig should try to break out of the circle of dogs, because such a pig, especially if wounded, is very dangerous. In a few minutes, however, the death of the pig was announced and I too plunged into the thicket to have a look. The first blow had apparently been struck as usual by the host hunt leader, and subsequent blows by the other hunt leaders.

The pig was indeed dead, but the excitement was not over. Dogs were snarling at the pig and at each other as they tore at the carcass. The hunters who gathered around encouraged the dogs by jerking the pig so that it moved, slashing it to make the wounds easier for the dogs to tear at, jabbing sticks into the wounds to collect blood

Altogether, it was a scene of considerable ferocity.

for the dogs on the periphery to lick. Eventually, the pig was dragged into the open and its limbs cut off and pulled about by the hunters to keep the dogs in a frenzy. Altogether it was a scene of considerable ferocity.

There was no formal closing of the hunt. Most hunters returned to the starting point, but others stopped to wash their dogs in a stream, have refreshment, or take a shortcut home. Our bus was several hours late, so all of us were tired and hungry by the time we finally began the trip back to Bayur. Perhaps because it had been a long and not very successful day, we made only a token amount of noise as we passed in the night through the various villages. For most of this hunt crowd, it was off to work the next day as usual and then another hunt the following Sunday.

Throughout the hunt and on the long walk back to our starting point, men and dogs continued to harass the livestock we encountered. When we passed through forests, plantations, and fields outside the villages, dogs were often unleashed in order to chase goats—sometimes until they collapsed in terror—and to snap at water buffalo; when we came to villages, dogs were kept on the leash but were encouraged by their masters to threaten livestock. No domestic animals were in fact injured on this hunt, as the dogs were eventually called off or the harassed animals lifted to safety, but I was told later with a kind of pride that domestic animals, in one case a valuable monkey trained to collect coconuts, were sometimes killed. In these cases no compensation is paid to the owner if the incident happens outside the village during a scheduled hunt. Any farmer imprudent enough to let his livestock run loose on such a day must suffer the consequences. When hearing about this, I remarked that the pig hunt must be a considerable inconvenience to farmers. True, I was told, but that is the way pig hunts are conducted.

Some—perhaps most—of the pig hunters clearly relished the degree of license and the sense of power which their participation in the pig hunt gave them. Although throughout the hunt people and crops were not molested, the harassment of domestic animals, the freedom with which men knocked down coconuts in the plantations for their own refreshment, the appearance of the men themselves—armed, often in torn clothes, flushed, excited, and noisy—created the explicitly recognized image and, I think, the experience among hunters and bystanders alike of a band of barely constrained parewa sweeping out from the wilds of the forest and invading the villages.

The meaning of the hunt derives from more than this display of parewa behavior of barely constrained energy; it also derives from the meaning dogs and pigs have for the strongly Muslim Minangkabau. Minang recognize that both pigs and dogs are animals with which a proper Muslim should have as little contact as possible. Why, then, I asked, do they so assiduously hunt pigs? Partly, they replied, to kill a religiously prohibited animal; partly to protect crops; but mainly because pig hunting is a traditional Minang sporting activity.

However, the fact of the hunt becomes considerably more significant once it is realized that some pigs are special: they are being punished for once having led evil lives as human beings. Usually these are men and women who engaged in magic and sorcery (in the case of women, much of this magic is thought to attract men sexually). Certain of these who became pigs have an iron ring in their noses which, as long as they wear it, grants them invulnerability. (I did hear of humans who found such a ring, temporarily laid aside by the pig while it cooled itself in a stream. These men then went on to enjoy illustrious careers in the police, the military, or crime, by using the ring's power to confer invulnerability.)

A person who is given the form of a pig as punishment is thought to visit his kin within a few days after his death. The kin will recognize him in his animal form and will attempt to provide what surreptitious help they can. Hence, when a calf appeared instead of a pig on the hunt I attended, it was whispered about that those hunters who were kin of the pig originally scented had either changed it into a calf through magic, or had lured a calf into the area to distract the dogs and allow the pig to escape. When this incident was discussed later, I raised the possibility that this might have been an invulnerable pig. If that had been the case, I was told, perhaps the kinsman had created the diversion with the calf to protect the men and dogs from the pig.

The view that some pigs were once human is a belief that the

Minang themselves regard as running counter to Islamic teaching, in that it denies the orthodox Muslim doctrine that all human beings remain in the grave after death until general judgment, following which they go either to heaven or to hell. In an attempt partially to resolve this contradiction in belief, one man suggested that perhaps these magicians, sorcerers, and other evildoers who become pigs have first been judged by Allah and condemned to become pigs; then, following their death as pigs, they go to hell. For many Minang the prospect of being harried by dogs and killed as a wild pig is a strong deterrent to sinful behavior, especially when allied to the orthodox Muslim view of hell.

One of the curious aspects of the hunt is that many of the hunters, and especially the leaders of the hunt, are just the sort of individuals who themselves might conceivably become pigs. Nambo Samsir, for instance, was a regular pig hunter. (As stated earlier, to him the prospect of becoming a pig was sufficiently real that he had publicly expressed the hope that he be reborn not as a pig but as a tiger.) The hunt leader is chosen by the other hunters partly for his knowledge of hunting spells and magic; those who go on the hunt to protect their deceased kinsman by diverting the other hunters are obviously skilled in magic; parewa generally are thought to be versed in occult knowledge. Perhaps it is in some way a measure of their audacity, a display of bravado, that leads these men to become or continue as avid hunters. Apparently the realization that some pigs are "really" humans adds zest to the hunt and is a cause for general pleasure when the hunt leader and others who have the requisite skill identify a dead pig as a former human.

The distinction between dogs and people also becomes somewhat blurred in the context of the hunt. Minang men identify very closely with their favorite hunting dogs. There are frequent discussions about particular dogs, and the men are very clear about the characteristics that distinguish a good hunting dog. The most important of these are the courage and good nose to chase a pig by itself, if necessary, and a strong and distinctive bay so that its owner and others can readily identify it while it is giving chase. A man will talk with pride about the wounds his dog has sustained from pigs, as the mark of its courage. He will brag about how large were the offers to buy his dog which he declined, thus indicating, not only the value of the dog and the attachment between the dog and himself, but also the extent of his own resources, which allows him to resist such large offers. The sums involved in purchasing a dog can be large by Minang standards. (The largest offer—declined—of which I heard was 250,000 rupiah, or $625.) Men often commission local photographers to take pictures of themselves with their favorite dogs; they invest in very fancy collars and leashes and proudly display these during the hunt. On the hunt itself men share their lunches with dogs.

All the hunting dogs are male because, I was told, males are stronger. (A secondary reason is that females might distract the males.) As I watched the dogs straining on their leashes, often egged on by their masters to harass livestock or just striding through the village or along the forest paths, they seemed to me to be an almost literal extension of the male self. This identification is also suggested by the response to my question of why the Minang so value their dogs when, like the pigs they despise, dogs are objectionable to Islam. I was told that an exception is made for dogs because of their great loyalty to humans. (Incidentally, the Minang observe in a rather tongue-in-cheek way the religious prohibition against having commercial transactions concerning dogs by claiming that dogs are not bought or sold: they are "exchanged," usually for gold.)

The Minangkabau pig hunt seems to define for the Minang a minimally socialized male. The ambiguity concerning the nature of the distinction drawn between pigs, dogs, and people that appears in the pig hunt (an ambiguity that may be expressed in the fact of religious prohibition itself, cf. Douglas 1966) is utilized by the Minang both to express and to create certain kinds of experience—that of maleness, energy, and formlessness.

The pig hunt is not a refined, constrained activity—it involves little formality in dress or conduct. Instead there is a strong theme of violence—violence between men and pigs, dogs and pigs, dogs and dogs, and sometimes between men themselves as they brawl because of and during dog fights. In addition, there is the violence between the living and the dead, the unjudged and the judged, which, given the Minang view of pigs, is implicit in the pig hunt. The dominant values of the hunt are physical aggressiveness, courage, audacity—not the restraint, hesitance, and control of baso basi. The values of the hunt are those expressed by the parewa either as he accepts a challenge to fight or as, in concert with others, he violently defends the integrity of the village. I mentioned earlier an example of such violence in the case of the motorcyclist who struck a Bayur resident. Another example is the pursuit of suspected thieves in a village, especially if they are outsiders. Such a pursuit strikes the Western observer and locals alike as resembling the chase in a pig hunt.

But the pig hunt is more than a direct expression of individual energy and impulse; it is a collective activity, and one that rests on certain minimal constraints. It is preceded by formal speech and is under the direction of the hunt leader, who gives the command to release the dogs. (This command, incidentally, was used by Datuak Rajo Panghulu in his Bayur lecture as an example of the collective restraint on which Minang society rests.) The pig hunt is also a democratic activity, in that any male is welcome. Panghulu and parewa, men from different localities and kinship groups all hunt together without any distinction other than that between the hunt leader and the others.

Pigs, dogs, and men all meet in the forest, away from habitations, away from the structures and distinctions—the forms—of society. What they all have in common is their energy and their capacity for violence. But, after all, it is the men who must control themselves collectively in the hunt: the pig hunt *must* be collective. And in the context of the hunt, men master in different ways both dogs and pigs, and so differentiate themselves from these two, somewhat different, manifestations of animality. In this encounter is specified, experienced, and thus created, the thin but crucial distinction between sociality and asociality, humanity and bestiality. These are, to be sure, general themes, but they are general themes that Minangkabau recognize and discuss in their everyday lives when they talk about constraint and absence of constraint— baso basi and bebas—and when they talk about and encounter panghulu and urang sumando, hippies and parewa. What emerges from the pig hunt, I suggest, is a clear reiteration of the image and experience of what men are known fundamentally to be, and what constraint is known to be necessary if human beings are to be

significantly different from the animals they hunt and hunt with—
that is, if human society is to exist.[1]

If I am correct in regarding the pig hunt as an experiencing of
the narrowly averted chaos of bebas, then the ritual for the ascension of a new panghulu may be the experiencing of narrowly averted
paralysis in the enactment of the condensed social form of baso
basi.

For the ascension of Firdaus Datuak Bandaro, the panghulu of
Bayur sat in their full regalia, exchanging formal speeches, with
their knees flat on the sitting mats. Despite the discomfort both of
this position and of their heavy clothing, the panghulu voluntarily
sat hour after hour, formally discussing issues of all degrees of
magnitude. Some issues were as small as whether they should
permit themselves to smoke, eat, or open the window; some were
as large as to concern the role of the panghulu and adaik in Minangkabau society. Within the microcosm of the panghulu convened
within the ceremonial enclosure, all activity was subject to the
group constraint of consensus. Eating, talking, smoking, moving,
were brought under constraint so stringent as to be substantially
divorced from their physical, impulsive, habitual, and individual
sources. The constraint within the ceremonial enclosure was baso
basi at its most demanding.

In maximum contrast to the ascension is the pig hunt. There
one finds energy, barely controlled and largely expressed in the
forest away from human habitation; in the ascension ritual there
is control, barely energized and expressed within the village and
in a special enclosure inside a house, as far from the forest as
possible, both physically and conceptually. In the pig hunt men
scarcely concern themselves with the embodiment, perception,
interpretation, and validation of social form. In the ascension ritual,
on the other hand, the embodiment, perception, interpretation, and
validation of social form become not merely concerns but virtual
obsessions.

Together, the pig hunt and the ritual of ascension comprise more
than just a statement about Minangkabau life; they embody that

[1] Much of the discussion here, as well as the circumstances of the pig hunt,
suggests Turner's 1969 treatment of the liminal period in ritual and the phase of
human experience which he calls *communitas*.

everyday life in condensed and extreme form. Such a statement and enactment, because of their exaggeration, are didactically effective, and also demonstrate the outermost permissible limits of Minangkabau society. To exceed these limits would be to brook either anarchy or immobility; to remain within them is to control that energy in a social order both vital and veritable.

Chapter Eight
Conclusion

By examining the way the Minang lead and interpret their lives, I have been addressing the question of how they construct experience so that it has both form and meaning, and how they extract form and meaning from that experience. I have been addressing the question of how the Minangkabau build and interpret the texts which compose their culture.

Minangkabau value their social forms not only because they provide means for controlling energy and thus for creating order but because these forms are right, reasonable, and true in themselves—because they are adaik. "Adaik," according to one of the most widely known Minang aphorisms, endures because it "neither cracks in the sun, nor rots in the rain." Adaik has the indissoluble and veritable strength to bind people together—as the three cords bind—into a community: to bind in the way that social forms bind through constraint.[1]

Baso basi is so greatly valued, not only because as a set of forms which control energy it is disjunctive with basic human inclination, but because it is a part of adaik and therefore an aspect of the

1. This is, of course, not the only possible basis of social order. The Karavarans of Papua New Guinea, for instance, are preoccupied with constraining energy but give little importance to the particular forms through which energy is channeled (Errington 1974). In contrast to both Karavarans and Minangkabau, some groups in Western society think that energy should be controlled, not primarily by enforcing adherence to social forms, but by controlling the energy at its source through proper socialization. Such a view stresses the importance of creating the capacity for self-restraint on which respect for the rights of others, and so on, is thought to be based.

right, reasonable, and true. To ignore baso basi is to ignore for reasons of perversity, irrationality, or lapse in attention the fact that one is in society. (People regarded as crazy usually do not display baso basi, nor is baso basi more than sporadically proffered to them.) Once, when a group of men and I were all sitting cross-legged, I noted that most of them were holding one knee at a right angle to the floor. Correctly taking this to indicate the informality of the occasion, I relaxed and in so doing put both my knees together at a right angle to the floor. After a few minutes, several of my companions remarked to me that they had all thought I must be distraught, so lost in a problem that I had forgotten I was still in the presence of others.

Interpretation of social forms is so greatly valued by the Minang because it incorporates both the recognition and the validation of form. Interpretation for them does not consist in simplification, transformation, or reduction, but in replication through showing correspondence of form. The replication usually consists either in pairing a form or aspect of form with another form or aspect of form which is regarded as true, or in pairing an aphorism with an actual situation. These pairings take the form of illustration and analogy.

Some of these pairings directly show not only that the forms of daily life exist, but that they are true, since they are congruent with the original forms of Minang life. Other comparisons, those which less obviously hold that contemporary forms are examples— illustrations—of original forms, are still based on the assumed truth or at least one member of the pair. When the comparisons are between contemporary forms, one or both forms illustrate the truth of the other. Bayur does, after all, have a mosque with four towers and, with only slightly less certainty, four categories of individuals. Through this kind of comparison, form is given truth. The situation is only slightly different when the comparison is between an aphor-ism and some aspect of conduct. Many Minang aphorisms can be described as contentless truth.[2] That nature should be our teacher is one such often cited truth. It was, for instance, cited to me as the justification of a more specific figure of speech—that an anak

---

2. This point, suggested to me by Joanne Prindiville, was based on her own Minangkabau research.

buah checks in with his panghulu just as a bird alights on a branch. Through these specific figures of speech the more general truth that nature should be our teacher is given form and substance. Through these various comparisons in which one member is seen as the replication of the other, truth is confirmed, reinforced, and given tangibility, while at the same time social form is recognized and given intelligibility and significance.

Minang define someone who has intellectual competence in adequate measure—who is a Minang at all—as being *arih*.[3] Someone who is arih can grasp quickly the meaning of an illustration or analogy, can grasp the essential contours of form. Arih, thus, is an important aspect of the Minang conception of themselves as oblique. Arih itself is described through analogies: when a fish flashes by in the water, one who is arih can tell what kind of fish it is or, in some versions of the analogy, whether the fish is male or female. Those who are arih have the competence to show that forms are at least fundamentally equivalent and can thereby also show that the particular social forms of contemporary life are right, proper, and reasonable, even when these have changed in certain respects from the original. (As Datuak Rajo Panghulu said, formerly one went to Jakarta by sailing ship; now one travels by steamship.)

There does not seem to me to be anything very much like symbols in this style of interpretation but only illustrations and analogies of varying degrees of size and complexity. The ritual of ascension for a panghulu is susceptible to the same kind of sign-oriented interpretation as anything else: the six streamers that figured in the ascension were interpreted in the same way as the five sides of the kaban or the four mosque towers. The regalia worn by the panghulu were interpreted to me in a similar way: the layers in the panghulu's turban refer to his elevation over his anak buah; the set of ridges in his kris refers to the layers in his turban; the representation of a peering bird on the handle of his kris refers to the close watch a panghulu keeps on his anak buah; and so forth.

The importance of the ritual of ascension—and the pig hunt— is not that they point to a part of reality, a layer of meaning, different

3. I am again indebted to Joanne Prindiville for her observation that this competence is central to the Minangkabau self-definition.

from that which Minang normally experience. Rather, their significance lies in the particularly compelling way in which they
present reality: they compel because they are enacted and involve
the participation of large numbers of people for major periods of
time. Most important, they compel because what is enacted is a
sufficiently large and condensed piece of adaik—a sufficiently substantial portion of social form as truth—to act as a major reference
point. As such, the ritual of a panghulu's ascension brings together
and makes both memorable and more true what the Minangkabau
already know to be the case about the significance of constraint
and the continuity of form—their particular brand of indirection—
in social life: the nature of baso basi, the nature of the relations
of panghulu to each other and to their anak buah, the nature of
the community—in other words, the nature of different forms of
obligation. The pig hunt brings together and makes both memorable
and additionally true what the Minang already know to be the case
about the significance of energy—the direct expression of freedom
and inclination—in social life: their capacity for violence, anger,
malice, as well as striving, productivity, development, and
friendship.

Although these are in both cases the well-understood themes of
everyday life, the Minangkabau are more likely spontaneously to
discuss the ritual of ascension than they are the pig hunt. This is
not to deny that they have quite a bit to say about the pig hunt.
Yet the fact remains that one of these two major reference points
does seem to be easier for them to talk about than the other. I can
see several mutually compatible reasons why this might be the
case. One lies in the preferred style of interpretation itself, which
proceeds by interpreting social form in terms of other social forms.
The Minangkabau are able to define and present examples of chaos
or near chaos (as in their discussions of the freedom from constraint
that is bebas); it is, however, perhaps rather more difficult for them
to present an analysis in terms of formal characteristics of institutionalized chaos, institutionalized formlessness. There is another
possible reason: they recognize that some of the beliefs central to
the pig hunt run counter to those of Islam, and that the pig hunt
is regarded as objectionable by the religious scholars of the community. Yet another possible reason might lie in the disquiet that

a recognition of the human capacity for disorder can arouse. However, whether it is for these or for still other reasons that the Minangkabau talk relatively little about the pig hunt, it is not, I think, because they find its meaning less than apparent.

Replications of any scale—ranging from isolated illustrations and analogies to large-scale enactments—create a mesh between ethos and world view. (This mesh, the coherence, *between* ethos and world view seems more important for the Minang to affirm than the mesh, the coherence, *within* ethos and *within* world view.) Because their lives are (should be) replications of adaik,[4] morality is reality. Because their interpretations of their lives rely on replication—through illustration, analogy, and enactment—the form of the interpretation itself generates the conviction of truth—or at least that there is truth—by its continual reference to adaik, the locus of reality. As a consequence, not only does morality mesh with reality but aesthetics does with ethics, to give the Minangkabau a sense of sureness about the way in which they not only lead but appraise their lives.

In my comparisons of Minangkabau consciousness with what I broadly conceive to be contemporary Western consciousness, I have argued that each contains a distinctive aesthetic about the nature of persons and of society. Each entails a different expectation about where meaning can be found, about the relationship of appearance—that is, immediate experience—and reality. And each consciousness contains a correspondingly different expectation about what form an adequate explanation would take: for the Minangkabau, explanation is through replication; for the Westerner, through reduction. There seems to exist a spectrum of culturally preferred styles of interpretation that would include little or no interpretation at all and corresponds to the cultural perception of the degree to which appearance and reality, immediate experience and truth, are proximate. If appearance and reality coincide—if things are what they seem—then the world is translucent; there is seldom need to engage in explicit interpretation, for meaning rarely needs to be represented—abstracted. Such is the case

---

4. This does not imply that there is no latitude for maneuvering within the social forms.

for the Karavarans of Papua New Guinea, and consequently signs and symbols, because they are modes of representation rather than (Karavaran) reality itself, are largely alien to Karavaran consciousness (Errington 1974).[5]

If, on the other hand, appearance and reality have become distant—if the world is opaque—then persons and events can convincingly be shown to have meaning only through interpretations which reduce the significance of immediate experience. By regarding immediate experience as alluding to, as symbolizing, an obscure yet what is hoped to be substantial reality, Western consciousness struggles to reconstitute truth.

If appearance and reality approach each other but do not coincide—if the world is only somewhat murky—then immediate experience does not seriously mislead, and signs are perfectly adequate for the construction of meaning. The Minangkabau, both in their interpretations and in their lives, can still reasonably aspire to the replication of reality and truth.

I wish finally to suggest some reasons why interpretive styles change. This requires that I briefly examine how and why social context changes to make appearance and reality seem increasingly divergent and, correspondingly, why the meaning of persons and social forms seems increasingly elusive.

The best way to approach this question, in my view, is to focus on the circumstances which could lead to the development of the concept of subjectivity, a development which leads to the distinction central to modern Western thought between subjectivity and objectivity, opinion and fact. In Western thought and experience, the subjective refers to an inward and unique self and to the unique perspective this self has. Subjectivity, then, is a cultural concept which both defines the self and describes how that self interprets and experiences the larger reality.

5. For the Karavarans, persons are what they do. Although they will note that a man is a chronic gossip or cigarette smoker, no one is interested in why he has these characteristics. A man who smokes a lot of cigarettes is a man who smokes a lot of cigarettes. Comparably (within some limits), social order—society—is Karavarans acting in an orderly way; ritual figures are, and mean, what ritual figures do (Errington 1974).

Cultures like the Karavaran lack such a concept of subjectivity. Karavarans define themselves as persons primarily through social position, determined by an interlocking set of criteria such as sex, kinship, political power, ritual prerogatives, and use of shell money. Definition of person through such evident and essentially social criteria rather than through the existence of an inner and largely personal self is described, or at least suggested, in a number of accounts of tribal societies. (For some examples, see Read 1967, Barton 1963, Gearing 1970.) Moreover, such cultures as that of the Karavarans are not likely to have a highly developed concept of perspective, as for them there are not *views* of reality, there simply *is* reality. Persons and social forms are as they appear; meaning is generally evident.

Horton (1967) describes the kind of cultural contact which may lead a culture like the Karavaran to recognize that there are various views of reality, that these views of reality may differ fundamentally, and that at least some of these differing views are potentially plausible. Once this happens, once a "closed" culture begins to "open," its members find it difficult to assume that the way in which they are accustomed to act and think is the only right, proper, and reasonable—the only realistically conceivable—way to act and think. Such a realization is likely to make them more self-conscious in making their interpretations of reality; it leads them to attempt justification of their particular cultural perspective. An innocent ethnocentrism may thus be replaced by a more wary and resourceful ethnocentrism, as members of a culture struggle to be cosmopolitan in a provincial sort of way or, in some cases, struggle to pretend that a very different outside world with its diverse perspectives does not, in any meaningful way, exist. Geertz (1968) also describes such responses, aptly characterizing them as the "struggle for the real."

The same struggle to maintain a sense of cultural certainty may be exacerbated by the acquisition of literacy (Goody and Watt 1968). Written texts not only may convey the perspectives of other cultures but, in the form of historical records, may suggest that one's own culture has significantly changed over time. When this happens, the past and the present can no longer be regarded as fundamentally commensurate, and present practices may need justification because they no longer appear unimpeachably reasonable by virtue of unbroken precedent.

Moreover, as it becomes more difficult to decide how to act and how to interpret under such circumstances, the social world is at the same time likely to become more complex, more difficult to interpret from any perspective. The kind of encounter between cultures that is likely to bring awareness of alternatives in perspective may also bring with it an increase in the complexity of the division of labor, in the importance of social class, in the variety of ethnic and religious groups, and in the extent of social and spatial mobility. As the social world becomes more confused, it becomes a less satisfactory context for providing the definition of person. As individuals confront the possibility that society is a historically contingent and changing set of conventions rather than a pattern of inherently reasonable social forms inextricably wedded to an unchanging reality, they are likely to find it ever more difficult to derive their own fundamental identity, and that of others, from social position.

Minangkabau culture is sufficiently open to recognize the existence of views of reality and modes of social order that are very different from their own. However, they still respond vigorously to the challenge provided by these alternative views and social orders by denying them plausibility. They respond to these threats to their conceptual and social order by making a concerted effort to maintain both a largely traditional view of the world and a primarily social definition of person. Minang are self-conscious in their interpretation and justification of adaik, maintaining uniformity of perspective through consensus; and they are preoccupied with ensuring that individuals continue to be defined socially—according to their conformity to baso basi and adaik, as members of a particular community, as anak buah of a particular panghulu. To the extent that Minang are successful in maintaining their particular balance between freedom and constraint, change and continuity, their world will appear sufficiently ordered as to be intelligibly interpreted through signs.

Modern Western culture, in my view, generally acknowledges diversity of perspectives and instability of social context. Not only does personal identity move inward to the subjective self, personally significant social reality has contracted as well. In the modern industrial West, it is the private realm of home, family, and love where individuals are most likely to seek, express, and experience their real selves. (See Henry 1963, Schneider 1968, Laing 1965, for instance, for discussions of aspects of this process.) In the West, then, to understand what another person really is requires a penetration of the public presentation of the self to probe at a largely hidden subjectivity. This is an intellectual operation similar in nature and in difficulty to finding pattern in a complex and shifting social world. Inherent is the danger that effort to arrive at objectivity will be tainted by the intrusion of personal perspective, subjectivity. There is also the danger that (mere) appearance misleads. Neither in the understanding of another person, nor in the understanding of the social world, can appearance and reality safely be assumed to coincide.

Glossary

adaik	All that is right and proper in indigenous Minangkabau society; Minangkabau custom
ambalau	Basic form of the ceremony of ascension to a panghulu title
anak buah	Matrilineal kin of a panghulu who are under his charge
bako	Matrilineal kin of an individual's father
baralek panghulu	Elaborate form of the ceremony of ascension to a panghulu title
baso basi	Good manners; Minangkabau etiquette
bebas	Freedom from constraint
carano	Brass urn used on ceremonial occasions
gotong royong	Help provided by the community at large
lalamak	Decorated cloth used on ceremonial occasions
panghulu	Matrilineage titleholder
parewa	A rowdy or a tough
payuang	Group of minor matrilineages sharing a panghulu title
periuak	Minor matrilineage
suku	Matriclan
urang sumando	Inmarried male

Bibliography

Abdullah, T. 1971. *Schools and Politics: The Kaum Muda Movement in West Sumatra (1927–1933)*. Monograph Series, Cornell Modern Indonesia Project, Southeast Asia Program, Cornell University, Ithaca, N.Y.

—————. 1972. "Modernization in the Minangkabau World: West Sumatra in the Early Decades of the Twentieth Century." In Claire Holt, Benedict Anderson, and James Siegel, eds., *Culture and Politics in Indonesia*. Ithaca, N.Y.: Cornell University Press.

Anderson, B. 1972. "The Idea of Power in Javanese Culture." In Claire Holt, Benedict Anderson, and James Siegel, eds., *Culture and Politics in Indonesia*. Ithaca, N.Y.: Cornell University Press.

Barton, R. 1963. *Autobiographies of Three Pagans in the Philippines*. New Hyde Park, N.Y.: University Books.

Brunton, R. 1980a. "Misconstrued Order in Melanesian Religion," pp. 112–28. *Man*, vol. 15, no. 1.

—————. 1980b. Correspondence: "Order or Disorder in Melanesian Religions?" pp. 734–35. *Man*, vol. 15, no. 4.

Dobbin, C. 1977. "Economic Change in Minangkabau as a Factor in the Rise of the Padri Movement, 1784–1830", pp. 1–38. *Indonesia*, no. 23.

—————. 1983. *Islamic Revivalism in a Changing Peasant Economy: Central Sumatra, 1784–1847*. London: Curzon Press.

Douglas, M. 1966. *Purity and Danger*. London: Routledge and Kegan Paul.

Dundes, A. 1980. "Into the Endzone for a Touchdown: A Psychoanalytic Consideration of American Football." In *Interpreting Folklore*. Bloomington: Indiana University Press.

Errington, F. 1974. *Karavar: Masks and Power in a Melanesian Ritual*. Ithaca, N.Y.: Cornell University Press.

Gearing, F. 1970. *The Face of the Fox*. Chicago: Aldine.

Geertz, C. 1968. *Islam Observed: Religious Development in Morocco and Indonesia*. Chicago: University of Chicago Press.

———. 1973. *The Interpretation of Cultures*. New York: Basic Books.

Gell, A. 1980. Correspondence: "Order or Disorder in Melanesian Religions?" pp. 735–37. *Man*, vol. 15, no. 4.

Goody, J., and I. Watt. 1968. "Consequences of Literacy." In J. Goody, ed., *Literacy in Traditional Societies*. Cambridge: Cambridge University Press.

Graves, E. 1981. *The Minangkabau Response to Dutch Colonial Rule in the Nineteenth Century*. Monograph Series, Cornell Modern Indonesia Project, Southeast Asia Program, Cornell University, Ithaca, N.Y.

Henry, J. 1963. *Culture against Man*, New York: Vintage Books.

Horton, R. 1967. "African Traditional Thought and Western Science," pp. 155–87. *Africa*, vol. 37, no. 2.

Johnson, R. 1981. Correspondence: "Order or Disorder in Melanesian Religions?" pp. 472–74. *Man*, vol. 16, no. 3.

Jorgenson, D. 1981. Correspondence: "Order or Disorder in Melanesian Religions?" pp. 470–72. *Man*, vol. 16, no. 3.

Jullierat, B. 1980. Correspondence: "Order or Disorder in Melanesian Religions?" pp. 732–34. *Man*, vol. 15, no. 4.

Laing, R. D. 1965. *The Divided Self*. Baltimore: Pelican Books.

Langer, S. 1942. *Philosophy in a New Key*. Cambridge, Mass.: Harvard University Press.

Kahn, J. S. 1981. *Minangkabau Social Formations: Indonesian Peasants and the World-Economy*. Cambridge: Cambridge University Press.

Kato, T. 1982. *Matriliny and Migration: Evolving Minangkabau Traditions in Indonesia*. Ithaca, N.Y.: Cornell University Press.

Mrazek, R. 1972. "Tan Malaka: A Political Personality's Structure of Experience," pp. 7–48. *Indonesia*, no. 14.

Naim, M. 1973. "Merantau: Minangkabau Voluntary Migration." Ph.D. dissertation, University of Singapore.

Phillips, N. 1981. *Sijobang: Sung Narrative Poetry of West Sumatra*. Cambridge: Cambridge University Press.

Prindiville, J. 1979. "Food, Form and Femininity: Minangkabau Women as Culinary Communicators." Unpublished.

Read, K. 1967. "Morality and the Concept of Person among the Gahuku-Gama." In J. Middleton, ed., *Myth and Cosmos*. Garden City, N.Y.: The Natural History Press.

Schlesinger, A. 1946. *Learning How to Behave: A Historical Study of American Etiquette Books*. New York: MacMillan Company.

Schneider, D. 1968. *American Kinship: A Cultural Account*. Englewood Cliffs, N.J.: Prentice Hall.

Schrieke, B. 1955. "The Causes and Effects of Communism on the West Coast of Sumatra." *Indonesian Sociological Studies: Selected Writings*, part 1. The Hauge: van Hoeve.

Siegel, J. 1969. *The Rope of God*. Berkeley: University of California Press.

Sontag, S. 1970. "Against Interpretation." In S. Sontag, *Against Interpretation*. New York: Farrar, Straus and Giroux.

Tanner, N. 1971. "Minangkabau Disputes." Ph.D. dissertation, University of California, Berkeley.

Turner, V. 1967. "Symbols in Ndembu Ritual." In V. Turner *The Forest of Symbols*. Ithaca, N.Y.: Cornell University Press.

———. 1969. *The Ritual Process*. Chicago: Aldine.

Index